# A
# **CATHOLIC**
# GUIDE TO
# Narnia

## QUESTIONS AND ACTIVITIES FOR
### *The Lion, the Witch and the Wardrobe*

ASCENSION

West Chester, Pennsylvania

Ascension
Post Office Box 1990
West Chester, PA 19380
1-800-376-0520
ascensionpress.com

Cover and interior design: Stella Ziegler
Printed in the United States of America
ISBN 978-1-950784-73-8

21 22 23 24 25 5 4 3 2 1

# CONTENTS

# Introduction

When C.S. Lewis first penned *The Chronicles of Narnia: The Lion, the Witch and the Wardrobe*, many critics felt that it was "too Christian" for the times, that fantasy literature wasn't popular with young readers, and that it depicted too much violence. Surprisingly, even Lewis' own publisher doubted whether the novel would sell and thought, perhaps, it would ruin the reputation of the author. However, against all expectations, Lewis' story of the fantastical world of Narnia with figures from Greek and Roman mythology, talking animals, Father Christmas, and tales of heroic deeds proved to be an immediate success. In fact, in the seventy years since it was published, it has sold over ninety-five million copies, has been translated into forty-seven languages, and has been adapted three times for television, six times for theatre, and three times for audio drama. In 2005, it was made into a feature film by Walt Disney Pictures and Walden Media, and, in 2019, it was listed by *Time* magazine as one of the 100 best novels of all time.

It is safe to say that the critics greatly misjudged the novel's appeal. Even now, this children's fantasy novel remains as popular as ever with readers both young and old alike. Therefore, it is worthwhile to step back and ask why this timeless novel has proved to be so popular with all age groups for so many years and why it still resonates with readers today.

Certainly, C.S. Lewis, a professor of literature at both Oxford University and Cambridge University, and arguably one of the greatest and most influential writers of the twentieth century, was an incredible storyteller. But is a "good story" all that there is to the world of Narnia? The answer lies in comparing Lewis' stories to those of another master storyteller, who told stories about mustard seeds, lost coins, and fields of tares and wheat—themes and subjects that were familiar to his listeners but that contained a much deeper meaning.

Like the New Testament parables, the stories about the world of Narnia convey eternal truths about the human condition. In fact, the world of Narnia is strikingly similar to our own. There is a creator and his creation, a tempter and the fall, temptation and sin, bravery and cowardice, loyalty and betrayal, and, perhaps most importantly, sacrifice and redemption. Even the characters in Narnia, like Aslan and the White Witch, are thinly veiled images of the protagonist and antagonist of the Christian story. Who wouldn't immediately see the similarities between Aslan, who sacrificed himself for the traitorous Edmund and then came back to life, and Christ, who offered himself as a sacrifice for our sins and rose again three days later. Indeed, the entirety of the Christian message can be found in the world of Narnia—and, like the characters in Narnia, we are called to choose sides in the great battle.

Readers of the New Testament often marvel that the disciples so often misunderstood the parables and that Christ would have to take them aside and explain the "deeper meaning." Fortunately for us today, there is nothing "hidden" in the parables because we have the reliable guide of apostolic teaching—the Magisterium—to explain what Jesus meant. In a similar way, it is helpful to have a guide that explores the "deeper meaning" of the stories and characters of Narnia. This is what *A Catholic Guide to Narnia: Questions and Activities for The Lion, the Witch and the Wardrobe* is intended to do—to connect the dots that show how the stories of Narnia relate to the human experience and the Christian message.

This revised edition presents several new features that are intended to aid Catholic families in learning more about C.S. Lewis, *The Lion, the Witch and the Wardrobe*, and the world of Narnia. These features can be found in the "Dive Deeper" section at the end of each chapter and include relevant quotations from Scripture and the *Catechism*, "Find It" questions for comprehension, and discussion questions to spark family conversations about the themes of the book and how they relate to our everyday experiences and the Catholic Faith. Each chapter also contains activities: the first is normally a "hands-on" activity for younger family members, the second is aimed at older readers, and a "For Further Exploration" section is for those seeking additional information about the themes discussed in the novel.

It is our hope at Ascension that this book will be a great aid for Catholic families who love the world of Narnia, will assist them to further discover the incredible riches of Christian truth that C.S. Lewis conveys through his stories, and will help them to discuss these themes and how they apply in our own world.

# CHAPTER 1

# About The Chronicles

**1)   What is *The Lion, the Witch and the Wardrobe*?**

*The Lion, the Witch and the Wardrobe* is the first of the seven *Chronicles of Narnia*, written by C.S. Lewis. It is a wonderful story that has entertained children and adults alike for over seventy years. It tells the tale of how Lucy, Edmund, Susan, and Peter Pevensie step into a magic wardrobe—a large closet-like cabinet that is used to hang clothes—through which they enter the land of Narnia and, with the help of the great Lion Aslan, deliver it from the enchantment of the White Witch. It is a story of excitement and adventure, honor and betrayal, good and evil, life and death—and resurrection. The stories, in addition to being a rollicking good read, portray aspects of Christianity in a way that younger children can understand and that adults can profit from as well.

## 2) Who was C.S. Lewis?

C.S. ("Clive Staples") Lewis (1898–1963) was one of the most famous and widely read Christian writers of the twentieth century. As a child, he and his brother invented the world of "Boxen," a land of talking animals. As he grew older, he developed a love of fantasy literature, fed in particular by the nineteenth-century fantasy writer George MacDonald, whom Lewis referred to as "my master."

As a professor of medieval and Renaissance literature at Oxford and Cambridge universities, Lewis wrote many academic works. He achieved his greatest fame and accomplishment as an apologist for the Christian faith and as a writer of children's novels, science fiction, and fantasy. His thoughtful, everyday explanations of Christianity are still widely read and have helped many understand and deepen their faith.

Born and raised in Belfast, Northern Ireland, Lewis abandoned Christianity as a teenager and declared himself an atheist. After much reading, searching, and the influence of his Oxford friends (including J.R.R. Tolkien, who played a pivotal role in his conversion to faith in Christ), Lewis came to a belief in God and ultimately became a Christian at the age of thirty-three. For the rest of his life, in addition to maintaining his full academic duties, Lewis wrote books on Christian theology and the Christian life that were instrumental in helping many to embrace Christianity or at least come to a more vibrant understanding of it. In *Mere Christianity*, for example, Lewis sought "to explain and defend the belief that has been common to nearly all Christians at all times," thus enabling them to embrace a clear explanation of the Christian faith.

Lewis' love of fantasy and his towering gifts as a writer of imagination, humor, wisdom, clarity, and beauty can be seen not only in his theological works but also in his fiction.

From *The Screwtape Letters* (a look at human temptation via an imaginary correspondence between a senior devil named Screwtape and his apprentice, Wormwood) to his celebrated "Space Trilogy" (three science fiction novels set on Mars, Venus, and Earth) to *The Great Divorce* (a look at damnation and beatitude via a bus ride from hell to heaven), Lewis has enthralled readers with his wonderful stories for more than eighty years. In the 1950s, Lewis began writing his most popular books—a series of fantasies for children, collectively known as *The Chronicles of Narnia*. The first book in the series, *The Lion, the Witch and the Wardrobe* proved to be so popular that Lewis began work on six sequels. All told, the seven books of *The Chronicles* have sold more than one hundred million copies worldwide. Christian concepts can be found throughout the stories.

**3)  Where is Narnia?**

Narnia, like Middle Earth of J.R.R. Tolkien's *Lord of the Rings* trilogy, is a fictional world. It is a land filled with talking animals, mythical creatures, and magic.

The geography of Narnia is mostly forest, with hills rising into low mountains in the south and marshlands in the north. To the east of Narnia lies the Eastern Ocean, to the west rises a great mountain range, to the north flows the River Shribble, and to the south lies the land of Calormen.

The Great River is at the center of Narnia, and it flows from the northwest on an east-southeasterly course to the Eastern Ocean. Narnia is ruled from the castle of Cair Paravel, at the mouth of the Great River.

**4)  Are *The Chronicles of Narnia* a Christian series?**

Yes and no. Although the seven books were not written as explicitly Christian works, the characters and events found within them often reflect Christian themes. As C.S. Lewis himself once remarked, "The whole Narnian story is about

Christ. That is to say, I asked myself, 'Supposing that there really was a world like Narnia and supposing it had (like our world) gone wrong and supposing Christ wanted to go into that world and save it (as he did ours) what might have happened?'"

We can see parallels to the Gospel throughout *The Chronicles*. For example, the hero of the series, Aslan the Lion, dies, comes back to life, and ultimately saves Narnia. The author uses the figure of a lion for Jesus because the lion is the king of the animals, and also because the Old Testament refers to the Messiah as the "lion of Judah."

The story of Narnia reflects Christian salvation history: *The Magician's Nephew* deals with creation and the entrance of evil into Narnia; *The Lion, the Witch and the Wardrobe* alludes to the death and resurrection of Jesus; *Prince Caspian* shows how true religion was corrupted and then restored; and *The Last Battle*, the final book, describes how an "antichrist" character, Shift the Ape, tries to take over Narnia, which leads to Aslan's second coming.

Most children, though, will probably not pick up on much of this symbolism—for them, Narnia is just an exciting story in which heroes win out over villains and good conquers evil in dramatic fashion.

## 5)  Is there a specific order that one should read *The Chronicles*?

As we shall see, time in Narnia and time in our world don't always line up. In a funny way, this is reflected in the order of the books. In our world, *The Lion, the Witch and the Wardrobe* was written in 1950. It was followed by the other *Chronicles* in this order:

- *Prince Caspian* (1951)

- *The Voyage of the Dawn Treader* (1952)

- *The Silver Chair* (1953)

- *The Horse and His Boy* (1954)
- *The Magician's Nephew* (1955)
- *The Last Battle* (1956)

However, in terms of Narnian history, the sequence is:

- *The Magician's Nephew*
- *The Lion, the Witch and the Wardrobe*
- *The Horse and His Boy*
- *Prince Caspian*
- *The Voyage of the Dawn Treader*
- *The Silver Chair*
- *The Last Battle*

None of this matters much. As C.S. Lewis states in a 1957 letter written to an American boy named Laurence:

I think I agree with your order [i.e. chronological] for reading the books more than with your mother's. The series was not planned beforehand as she thinks. When I wrote *The Lion* I did not know I was going to write any more. Then I wrote *P. Caspian* as a sequel and still didn't think there would be any more, and when I had done *The Voyage* I felt quite sure it would be the last. But I found I was wrong. So perhaps it does not matter very much in which order anyone reads them. I'm not even sure that all the others were written in the same order in which they were published (from *Letters to Children*).

**6)  Have any of *The Chronicles of Narnia* books ever been made into movies?**

Yes. In 2005, the first novel of the series, *The Chronicles of Narnia: The Lion, the Witch and the Wardrobe,* was made into a feature film by Walt Disney Pictures and Walden Media. Three years later, in 2008, they released the film adaptation of the second novel, *The Chronicles of Narnia: Prince Caspian.* The third novel of the series, *The Chronicles of Narnia: The*

*Voyage of the Dawn Treader,* was adapted for film and released by Walden Media and 20th Century Fox in 2010. These films have been faithful to the original books. Of course, as with any filmed adaptation of a novel, the screenwriters and directors have changed some details to enhance the story's dramatic and visual effect. But the movies essentially portray the stories as C.S. Lewis originally wrote them.

## DIVE DEEPER
### Bible and *Catechism* Connections

*With many such parables he spoke the word to them, as they were able to hear it; he did not speak to them without a parable, but privately to his own disciples he explained everything.*
**—Mark 4:33-34**

*Jesus' invitation to enter his kingdom comes in the form of parables, a characteristic feature of his teaching (cf. Mk 4:33–34). Through his parables he invites people to the feast of the kingdom, but he also asks for a radical choice: to gain the kingdom, one must give everything (cf. Mt 13:44–45; 22:1–14).*
**—CCC 546**

## FIND IT

1. How many books are in *The Chronicles of Narnia* series? Which was the first written?
2. What was the world of "Boxen"?
3. What subjects did C.S. Lewis teach at Oxford and Cambridge?
4. Who played a pivotal role in the conversion of C.S. Lewis?
5. Briefly describe the land of Narnia.

# TALK IT OUT

1.  Reading good books and the influence of good friends helped C.S. Lewis to become a Christian. Discuss how good books and good friendships can help us to be better Christians.

2.  Discuss some of the ways in which *The Chronicles of Narnia* is a Christian series. What are some ways in which it is not a Christian series?

3.  C.S. Lewis did not write *The Chronicles of Narnia* in chronological order (in the order that they occur in Narnia). In what order do you think *The Chronicles of Narnia* series should be read—chronologically or in the order that C.S. Lewis wrote them? Why?

# ACTIVITY

## Prodigal Son Skit

In this activity, you will need three people to play the parts of the father, the elder son, and the prodigal son. If there are more people, one could play the part of the narrator, and the others could help with props, which could include a bag of money, corn, a ring, and a robe. Read aloud the Parable of the Prodigal Son found in Luke 15:11-32. The actors should have a few minutes to discuss how they are going to perform the skit, and, if time allows, they could make some notes and practice beforehand. Afterward, discuss what Jesus was trying to tell us through the parable about the forgiving nature of God, how we should act when we do something wrong, and how we should treat other people when they say they are sorry.

# ACTIVITY
### Rewriting or Retelling the Parables

Jesus taught his followers by telling parables—stories that used simple images and ideas familiar to his listeners. In a similar way, C.S. Lewis taught many Christian truths through storytelling. Read the Parable of the Good Samaritan (see Luke 10:25-37). Individually, or together, rewrite or retell the parable in a modern-day setting, using modern-day characters. If rewriting the parable, each person should read their parables aloud.

# FOR FURTHER EXPLORATION

C.S. Lewis was influenced by his good friend J.R.R. Tolkien. Research the biography of J.R.R. Tolkien. Who was he? What types of literature did he write? In what way might he have influenced C.S. Lewis? Have you read any of Tolkien's books or watched movies based on his books? If you have, do you think they could both be and not be a Christian story? Why or why not? Which of Tolkien's books might you like to read next?

# CHAPTER 2
# The Story Begins

### 7)  Why are the four children sent to the Professor's house?

Since it is 1940, World War II is raging and German bombs
are being dropped on London. For their own protection,
the children are sent far from their home in the city to
the Professor's large country house. During this dark and
dangerous period of history, many English families sent
their children out of the cities to stay in the relative safety of
the countryside.

### 8)  Who is the Professor?

Professor Kirke is Digory, the boy from *The Magician's Nephew*,
as an old man. He also appears at the happy ending of *The
Last Battle*.

In *The Magician's Nephew*, Digory's uncle makes magic rings
that allow their wearers to travel to other worlds by passing
through the "Wood between the Worlds." After leaving
the Wood and entering another world, Digory gives in to

temptation, breaks a magic spell, and releases Jadis (who will become the White Witch) from the dead world, Charn. He accidentally brings her back to London and, ultimately, to Narnia. As a boy, Digory represents the power of free will and its consequences.

**9)  How old are the children?**

We are never told the ages of any of the children, just that Lucy will be old enough to go to boarding school "next year." Fortunately, though, Lewis wrote out a timeline spanning 2,555 years of Narnian history from which we learn their ages at the time they enter Narnia through the wardrobe: Lucy turns eight that year; Edmund, ten; Susan, twelve; and Peter, thirteen.

# DIVE DEEPER
## Bible and *Catechism* Connections

*When the woman saw that the tree was good for food, and that it was a delight to the eyes, and that the tree was to be desired to make one wise, she took of its fruit and ate; and she also gave some to her husband, and he ate.*
**—Genesis 3:6**

*Scripture portrays the tragic consequences of this first disobedience. Adam and Eve immediately lose the grace of original holiness (cf. Rom 3:23). ... The harmony in which they had found themselves, thanks to original justice, is now destroyed. ...Harmony with creation is broken: visible creation has become alien and hostile to man (cf. Gen 3:17, 19). ... After that first sin, the world is virtually inundated by sin.*
**—CCC 399–401**

The Story Begins 15

# FIND IT

1. Why did Peter, Susan, Edmund, and Lucy leave their family to stay with strangers in the countryside?

2. Who is the Professor? What other books in *The Chronicles of Narnia* does he appear in?

3. In *The Magician's Nephew*, how do people travel between worlds?

4. Why did Digory break the magic spell? What happened when he did this?

5. How old are the children when they enter the Land of Narnia?

# TALK IT OUT

1. How do you think Peter, Susan, Edmund, and Lucy felt when they had to leave their parents in London to live with strangers in the countryside? How would you feel if you were separated from your parents?

2. The Professor lived in a very large, old, and famous house in the countryside. What do you think they thought when they first saw the house where they would be staying?

3. When Digory gives into temptation and breaks the magic spell, he releases Jadis, the White Witch, who will spread evil throughout the world. How is this similar to Adam and Eve, who gave into temptation and disobeyed God? What were the consequences of their actions?

# ACTIVITY
### Draw a Picture

The *Catechism* tells us that after the first sin of Adam and Eve, the entire world became full of sin. Draw a picture of the Tree of the Knowledge of Good and Evil. Make sure to put a lot of delicious-looking fruit on the tree. Next to each fruit write the name of a sin that we have in the world today as a result of Adam and Eve disobeying God and eating the forbidden fruit. If you need help, refer back to the Ten Commandments.

## ACTIVITY
### Write a Letter

When Adam and Eve disobeyed God, they brought sin and suffering into the world. This affected not only themselves but all future generations. However, God did not abandon them. In Genesis 3:15, he promises that there will be a woman whose Son will defeat the serpent. In a similar way, Digory gives into temptation and unleashes Jadis, the White Witch, who will inflict evil upon generations of Narnians. Write a letter to Digory, telling him not to give up hope because one day there will be four children who will defeat the White Witch with the help of Aslan. When finished, read your letter aloud.

## FOR FURTHER EXPLORATION

The nightly bombing of London during World War II is referred to as the Battle of Britain. Research how long the Battle of Britain lasted and how many children were sent from London to places of safety in other parts of the country. What was this evacuation of the children called? Why might it have been given that name? If you aren't familiar with the name, which comes from a classic folktale, take a few minutes to read it. Versions can be found online. In a similar way to *The Chronicles of Narnia,* this folktale tells a story with a simple moral, which can be found in the last line. What was the moral of the story? (Hint: The folktale is called *The Pied Piper of Hamelin.*)

CHAPTER 3

# After Lucy Goes
# Through the Wardrobe

## 10) Why does Lucy go into the wardrobe?

One rainy day when the children can't go outside to play,
they decide to explore the Professor's large house. They soon
come upon a room with nothing in it but a large, wooden
wardrobe. While the other three quickly run ahead, Lucy is
intrigued and wants to see what is inside, though she thinks
it will be locked. When the door opens easily, she goes in and
her adventure in Narnia begins, an adventure that will soon
involve all of her siblings as well.

## 11) What makes the wardrobe magical?

The wardrobe is magical because it is made of Narnian
wood. An explanation of this remarkable fact is found in the
first book of the series, *The Magician's Nephew*. Digory, the
"nephew" of the story, brought an apple back from Narnia and
planted the core in our world. Though the tree grew in our
world, its wood was Narnian, so it retained its magical power.
When the tree was blown down in a storm, the wardrobe was

made from its wood. It served as an entrance into Narnia three times: once for Lucy alone, then for Lucy and Edmund, and finally for all four children.

## 12) Why couldn't the children experience the magical power of the wardrobe unless "both feet were in"?

C.S. Lewis probably uses this as a metaphor for being totally committed to a particular path or course of action. In other words, the children cannot experience Narnia by keeping "one foot" in this world—they need to plunge totally into its magic.

Similarly, as Christians, we are called to follow Jesus with our whole hearts, minds, and souls. If we want to experience his grace in our lives and ultimately enter heaven, we must take up our crosses daily and follow him. Jesus has strong words for those who are "lukewarm" or "half-hearted" in their commitment to him (see Revelation 3:16). If we want to be holy, we can't keep "one foot in" the world; we need to keep both feet firmly planted in the kingdom of God.

## 13) What is a lamp-post doing in a forest in Narnia?

In *The Magician's Nephew*, we read about how Aslan created Narnia and how the lamp-post was grown from a bar that Jadis (the future White Witch) brought from London. It serves as a reference point for the children as they find their way through Narnia, helping point them in the right direction.

We can see how the lamp-post might be a symbol referring to Jesus, "the light of the world." In the light of the Gospel, Jesus reveals that we do not stumble in the darkness of our sins but walk in the light of God's truth.

## 14) Is the lamp-post significant to Christianity?

In Matthew 5:14-16, in the Sermon on the Mount, Jesus tells his disciples: "You are the light of the world. A city set on a hill cannot be hidden. Nor do men light a lamp and put it under a bushel, but on a [lamp] stand, and it gives light to all in the house. Let your light so shine before men, that they may see your good works and give glory to your Father who is in heaven."

The lamp-post is present in the Wild Woods of the West to give light to all who come into Narnia. Several good deeds take place in its light. Mr. Tumnus and Peter ask for Lucy's forgiveness there, and at the end of the four children's time in Narnia, they discuss all of the good they have accomplished and resolve that they must continue together to perform good works and follow the path set before them.

### 15) Who is the first character Lucy meets in Narnia?

The first Narnian creature Lucy meets is Mr. Tumnus, who is a faun. In Roman mythology, a faun is a creature that has the upper body of a man and the horns, ears, tail, and legs of a goat. Fauns live in untamed woodlands and forests. In Greek mythology, a faun is known as a satyr.

### 16) Why does the Faun, Mr. Tumnus, call Lucy a "daughter of Eve"?

We need to remember that none of the creatures in Narnia are human. Although Mr. Tumnus has never seen a human being, he calls Lucy a "daughter of Eve" because she is a girl and he knows that all humans are descendants of Adam and Eve. Also, there is a legend in Narnia that speaks of the "sons of Adam" and the "daughters of Eve."

In the popular devotional prayer Hail, Holy Queen, we pray, "To thee do we cry, poor banished children of Eve ..." Our Christian faith teaches that Eve is the mother of all the living, so women are her "daughters" and men are her "sons." We are "banished" due to original sin, and we ask Mary's help to resist temptation and grow in holiness.

## 17) How does Mr. Tumnus entice Lucy to go with him to his home?

Mr. Tumnus entices Lucy to his home by offering her things he knew she would enjoy: warmth from the cold, tea, and cake. While these things are good in and of themselves, Mr. Tumnus intends to use them for a bad end—namely, to hand Lucy over to the White Witch.

In a similar way, the seemingly innocent and harmless things of the world can distract us and ultimately turn us away from doing what is right. If we let ourselves love the world more than we love God, we will lose sight of our purpose and set ourselves up for trouble.

## 18) Who is the White Witch?

The White Witch is the chief villain of *The Lion, the Witch and the Wardrobe*. She is an evil creature who stole the throne of Narnia and cast a spell causing it to be "always winter and never Christmas." By the beginning of the book, the winter had lasted one hundred years.

We learn in *The Magician's Nephew* that her real name is Jadis and that her pale white appearance is caused by her eating a forbidden apple from the Emperor's Garden in Narnia at the beginning of that world. Only those who were instructed to take one of these apples could do so, and even then they could not eat it themselves but had to give it to another for their benefit. By eating an apple without permission, Jadis became evil, and her skin turned white. Her magical powers flow mostly from her wand, which allows her to turn creatures into stone.

Here we can see a parallel with the creation story in Genesis, specifically the sin of Adam and Eve in eating the forbidden fruit from the Tree of the Knowledge of Good and Evil (see Genesis, chapter 3). Their sin condemned them and all their descendants to a life of hard work, suffering, and death, when our bodies return to the dust of the earth (rather like turning to stone). It is only with the passion, death, and resurrection of Jesus that we have been reconciled with God and now have the hope of salvation and eternal life.

So the White Witch's "fall," like that of Satan, confirms her in a life of evil, always grasping at power and domination over the inhabitants of Narnia. She calls herself "Her Imperial Majesty Jadis, Queen of Narnia, Chatelaine of Cair Paravel, and Empress of the Lone Islands." It is also worth noting that, though entirely corrupt, she remains extremely beautiful. This recalls St. Paul's warning that "Satan disguises himself as an angel of light" (2 Corinthians 11:14).

### 19) Is the Witch human?

No, but she claims to be so she can rule over Narnia. At the creation of Narnia, Aslan gives "the sons of Adam and the daughters of Eve" the right to rule over all of its animals and magical creatures. By falsely claiming to be a "daughter of Eve," the White Witch can call herself Queen of Narnia.

Despite her unnatural skin color and above-average height, the White Witch *appears* to be human. She is actually descended from the Jinn (ugly and evil demons having supernatural powers that they can bestow on those who summon them) and the giants. This race once inhabited Charn, a dying world from which Jadis escapes in *The Magician's Nephew*.

### 20) Before the winter, we are told that the streams of Narnia flowed with wine rather than water. What is the meaning behind this?

This is a clear reference to the Gospel of John as well as to any number of pagan myths. At the wedding feast of Cana (see John 2:1-11), Jesus turns water in stone jars into wine. This is Jesus' first miracle, and with it he begins his public ministry and begins to reveal to the apostles who he is. Likewise, in Greek mythology (which Lewis loved), wine is the symbol of joy, abundance, and plenty, much as it is in the Psalms, as when the psalmist rejoices, "There are many who say, 'O that we might see some good! / Lift up the light of your countenance upon us, O LORD! / You have put more joy in my heart / than they have when their grain and wine abound'" (Psalm 4:6-7).

Narnia was created by Aslan as an idyllic and magical land, where different creatures live together in happiness and peace. Since wine is a drink of celebration and comfort, it is appropriate that Narnian streams would flow with wine before the winter caused by the wicked rule of the White Witch.

## 21)  What is wrong with the seasons in Narnia after the White Witch takes over?

After the White Witch seizes power and begins her illegitimate rule over Narnia, there is only one season: winter. So life is always cold and dreary, without any hope of the coming of the warmth and brightness of spring.

Theologically, the seasons mirror the cycle of life: the warmth and full bloom of summer can be seen to symbolize life at its full strength and vigor; autumn (or fall) is a reflection of life growing older and slower; the cold of winter, death; and spring, new life.

## 22)  Does the White Witch practice "white magic"?

You may hear some people make a distinction between so-called "white magic," which is used for the benefit of others, and "black magic," which is used to harm others. Because of this, you would think that a "white witch" would be one who practices white magic and is therefore good. In *The Chronicles*, however, "white" refers to snow, ice, and the cold of death. So, far from being good, the White Witch is a destructive force in Narnia. In addition, we are told that the color of the skin on her face and arms is a deathly white.

### 23) What does the White Witch represent?

She is a representation—a *personification*—of evil. Since she directly opposes Aslan, who is good, and everyone who follows him, she could be said to represent the devil, who desires to turn everyone against their ultimate good—God.

Like the devil, the White Witch's considerable powers are ultimately no match against the forces of good. In the end, she is destroyed by her own evil works.

### 24) Why doesn't Mr. Tumnus turn Lucy over to the White Witch?

Though he is in the service of the White Witch, Mr. Tumnus regrets this when he comes to see that Lucy, as a daughter of Eve, is good. He decides not to turn her over to the White Witch because he realizes this would be wrong. By making the decision to do what is right, Mr. Tumnus knows he may have to suffer the anger of the Witch and perhaps be turned into stone. Nonetheless, he is willing to risk his very life to see that Lucy gets home safely.

Mr. Tumnus, then, can be said to have had a conversion experience—by failing to hand Lucy over to the Witch, he turns away from serving evil to do a profoundly good deed.

### 25) Peter, Susan, and Edmund meet up with Lucy after she has been through the wardrobe and tell her she has only been gone a moment. Why is this?

In Lucy's experience, she spends many hours in Narnia with Mr. Tumnus. So she is very surprised when her siblings insist she has been gone only a moment.

Apparently, time in Narnia does not coincide with time on Earth. One can spend hours (or even years) in Narnia while no time at all elapses on Earth. But the nature of time in Narnia is apparently flexible; it is not always consistent. We can see this explained in *The Voyage of the Dawn Treader*: "If you went back to Narnia after spending a week here, you might find that a thousand Narnian years had passed, or only a day, or no time at all. You never know till you get there."

# DIVE DEEPER
## Bible and *Catechism* Connections

*God is faithful, and he will not let you be tempted beyond your strength, but with the temptation will also provide the way of escape, that you may be able to endure it.*
**—1 Corinthians 10:13**

*"Lead us not into temptation" implies a decision of the heart: "For where your treasure is, there will your heart be also. ... No one can serve two master" (Mt 6:21, 24). "If we live by the Spirit, let us also walk by the Spirit" (Gal 5:25).*
**—CCC 2848**

# FIND IT

1. Why is the wardrobe magical?

2. How is the lamp-post a symbol for Christ?

3. What does it mean that Lucy is a "daughter of Eve"? Why are Christians called "banished children of Eve"?

4. How did Jadis become evil? How is this similar to the story of the Fall of Adam and Eve?

5. How was Narnia before the winter similar to Eden before the Fall?

# TALK IT OUT

1. In Narnia, the four children couldn't experience the magic of the wardrobe unless they had "both feet" in. The author compares that to Christians, who are called to follow God with their whole hearts and minds. What are some ways in which we might only have "one foot" in as followers of Christ? What can we change in our lives in order to have "both feet" in?

2. Mr. Tumnus tempted Lucy to come to his house by offering her some food. What are some "good" things in our everyday lives that might distract us from God if we use them unwisely?

3. Mr. Tumnus does not turn Lucy over to the White Witch, even though he knows he may be punished. What are some examples in our own lives in which we must choose to do right even if it involves personal suffering?

# ACTIVITY
## Role Playing

When Lucy enters Narnia and meets Mr. Tumnus, he invites her back to his house. After sharing tea and sandwiches with her, he plays a tune that makes her sleepy. He is supposed to help the White Witch, who told him to bring her any human children he meets. In this role-playing activity, which requires three people, you will explore the struggle that Mr. Tumnus is having with his conscience. (Conscience is the interior voice that helps us know the difference between right and wrong.) One person should play Mr. Tumnus. The second person should play the role of a good angel, who should try to convince him to let Lucy go. The third person should play the role of the devil's advocate, who should try to convince him to turn Lucy over to the White Witch. In the alternative, a dialogue between the good angel, the devil's advocate, and Mr. Tumnus could be written.

## ACTIVITY
### Role Playing

Perform the same role-playing activity as above, but adapt it to
a real-life situation. For example, the temptation might be to
cheat on an exam, to steal a candy bar from a store, or to play a
video game that has been prohibited by one's parents. Reasons
for avoiding bad actions should go beyond "you might get caught"
and include the fact that sin harms our relationship with God
and with others. In the alternative, a dialogue between the good
angel, the devil's advocate, and the boy or girl could be written.

## FOR FURTHER EXPLORATION

Read 2 Peter 3:8 and CCC 600, which tell us that God's
"time" is very different from time as we experience it here
on earth. In what way is time in Narnia similar to time
in relation to God? In what way is it different? What does
the *Catechism* mean when it says, "To God, all moments
of time are present in their immediacy" (CCC 600)?

# CHAPTER 4

# After Edmund Goes Through the Wardrobe

**26) Why can't Edmund find Lucy in the wardrobe when they are playing hide-and-seek?**

At first, Edmund doesn't realize that the wardrobe is actually an entrance to Narnia. He fully expects Lucy to be hiding behind the coats. So he is very surprised to discover that not only is Lucy *not* in the wardrobe but that he has actually stepped into another world.

When she enters into Narnia the second time, Lucy runs directly to Mr. Tumnus' home without knowing that Edmund is following after her. When she gets to Tumnus' cave, Lucy is reassured to hear that the White Witch has done nothing to him for letting her go.

**27) Why does Edmund describe the Witch as beautiful?**

Because, in her own way, she *is* beautiful. We usually think of evil as being ugly, but the opposite is often true. Sin can be very attractive, beautiful, and enticing; for a time, it can mislead us into thinking that it is actually good. Edmund sees the Witch as beautiful not least because she promises to fulfill his selfish desires.

Sometimes we may suspect—or even know—that a particular desire or behavior is evil, but we still pursue it because it is appealing. We can let our sins blind us. The lesson here is that we must be careful to form our hearts and minds according to what God has *revealed* to be good and true in the Bible and the teachings of the Church. We should not allow apparent beauty or instant gratification to lead us astray.

### 28) What is Turkish Delight, the candy Edmund seems to love so much?

Turkish Delight is a candy made of jelly-like cubes flavored with rosewater and covered with powdered sugar. Edmund remarks that the pieces of Turkish Delight the Witch gave him were "sweet and light to the very center." In *The Lion, the Witch and the Wardrobe*, they are symbolic of sin: they are delicious at their first taste but totally unsatisfying in the end. In fact, consuming too much actually makes Edmund feel sick, yet he still craves more. We can see that Edmund's craving for more leads him to other sins and ultimately to betraying his family.

### 29) Why does the Witch ask Edmund whether there are other children with him?

Because she is very concerned about her future. As we later see in the story, there is a legend in Narnia that when two sons of Adam and two daughters of Eve sit on the four thrones at Cair Paravel, it will not only be the end of the White Witch's reign but also of her life. We should notice, though, that this prophecy requires the free will of those it concerns to be fulfilled, that is, Edmund is free to reject the Witch's will, the other children are free to reject their destiny, and all are free to accept or reject Aslan. At the same time, all these free choices are going to be woven together by Aslan to fulfill the prophecy.

## 30) Why does the Witch tell Edmund he can have all the Turkish Delight he wishes if he brings his brother and sisters to her castle?

Because she wants to capture and kill all of them to keep the prophecy from being fulfilled and thus protect her rule over Narnia. The lesson here is that there are always strings attached to evil and sin—and that the devil is a liar. We may not notice the strings right away, but we always do in the end. At first, everything seems wonderful: Edmund gets a warm drink while it is cold outside, and he eats the best Turkish Delight he ever tasted. Once he tastes it and is hooked, he wants more and is willing to do whatever he has to do in order to get what he wants. He is blind to the manipulation the Witch is using to get what she wants. Her manipulation is a twisted parody of the offering Aslan will make of himself, and of the loving response he will ask of his followers as he calls for courage in battle against evil.

## 31) Why does the Witch then tell Edmund she will crown him as High King? Isn't the Turkish Delight enough to get him to do her bidding?

Smaller sins lead to bigger ones. The Witch, by manipulating Edmund with the promise of being King, is leading him on from mere sins of the flesh to sins of the spirit, especially pride and envy. While the offer of more Turkish Delight might have been enough to get him to do her bidding, she chains his soul more profoundly by offering him more. She knows Edmund is resentful of Peter's role as the oldest, and she plays on this resentment with an offer for him to become ruler over all his siblings and, indeed, all of Narnia. Since we're told that Edmund has a mean streak and a selfish disposition, it is an offer he is too weak to refuse.

In the Witch's two-fold temptation of Edmund—with food and power—we can see a reflection of the devil's temptation of Jesus. In the Gospel, we read that Jesus, in preparation for the start of his public ministry, fasted and prayed for forty days and nights in the desert. So the devil tempts him to turn stones into bread. Jesus responds by saying, "Man does not live by bread alone but by every word that comes from the mouth of God." Then the devil promises Jesus power over all the kingdoms of the world if he falls down and worships him. This in turn reflects the temptation of Adam and Eve. The forbidden fruit has two aspects: It was "good for food" and "a delight to the eyes" (the appeal to appetite) and "was to be desired to make one wise" (the appeal to pride and the sins of the spirit). Jesus' response to Satan gives us a clear example of how we must respond when tempted to evil.

**32) Why doesn't Edmund suspect the Witch is on the wrong side, especially after she tells him to keep their conversation about him becoming High King a secret and not to believe the negative things he may hear about her?**

Edmund lets his selfish wants blind him to the truth about the Witch. He *needs* to convince himself she is good to justify his alliance with her; otherwise, he is knowingly committing himself to doing evil. When we choose to follow our own will rather than God's, we can talk ourselves into believing anything. Scripture refers to this as having a "darkened understanding" (Ephesians 4:18). As Lewis puts it in *The Magician's Nephew*, "The trouble about trying to make yourself stupider than you really are is that you very often succeed."

In the Garden of Eden, the serpent (representing the devil) tricks Eve by telling her that God doesn't want them to eat from the Tree of the Knowledge of Good and Evil because then they would be like God. She was being tempted and gave in to the serpent's lies. With her encouragement, Adam too sinned by eating the forbidden fruit. Remember—both of them had heard the voice of God himself and enjoyed his friendship. Even so, they disobeyed his commands out of pride. We too can be easily tricked by the devil into doing what is wrong if we do not listen to God's Word and pray for the grace to follow his will in our lives.

### 33)  Why is Edmund so mean to Lucy?

From the beginning of the story, Edmund is portrayed as having a negative attitude and temperament. Peter mentions that he has been "beastly" to the smaller kids at school. He is also negative about the weather when they first get to the Professor's home and it is raining outside. Then he continues to pick on Lucy after she returns from her first visit to Narnia and tells her story to the others. It seems Edmund has a tendency to want attention and power, so maybe he is jealous of Lucy's purity and innocence. Since she embodies what is good, Edmund probably feels a little uncomfortable being around her and so treats her badly. We should note, though, that these are all choices on Edmund's part. He is not "made that way." He *chooses* to be that way. And his bad choices lead to bigger choices with more serious consequences.

### 34)  Edmund hides the fact he has gone through the wardrobe from his siblings. Why does he do this?

He does this so he can manipulate Peter, Susan, and Lucy into going to the Queen's home once they all get to Narnia. If he says that he has been to Narnia already, then he admits to Peter and Susan that Lucy is right, and he is afraid that her stories about the Witch may sway Peter and Susan into not believing and following him once they are all in Narnia. For his own selfish reasons, he does not tell the truth.

### 35)  How does the Professor understand all about the nature of the world of Narnia?

The Professor knows much about Narnia's magic and mystery because he was the first Son of Adam—the first human boy—

to go to Narnia. At the end of the story, Aslan allowed Digory to take an Apple of Life back to his world to heal his mother from her terminal illness. After his mother ate the apple and was miraculously cured, Digory took the core and planted it in his garden. The core eventually grew into a great tree that bore the finest apples in England—and still contained the Narnian magic. When Digory was a middle-aged man (and a distinguished professor), it was blown down by a powerful storm. Not wanting it to be chopped up for firewood, the Professor had the wardrobe made from its wood.

**36)** **The Professor doesn't say much, but when Peter and Susan go and see him about Lucy, he addresses them very seriously. How does he answer their doubts about Lucy and her story about Narnia?**

The Professor tells the children there are only three possibilities: Lucy is either lying, "mad" (i.e., crazy), or telling the truth. Since there is no evidence of the first two possibilities, the Professor advises the children to consider the possibility that Lucy is speaking the truth.

Lewis, in his book *Mere Christianity*, makes a similar point about Jesus:

A man who was merely a man and said the sort of things Jesus said would not be a great moral teacher. He would either be a lunatic—on the level with the man who says he is a poached egg—or else he would be the devil of Hell. You must make your choice. Either this man was and is, the Son of God: or else a madman or something worse. You can shut Him up for a fool, you can spit at Him and kill Him as a demon; or you can fall at His feet and call Him Lord and God. But let us not come with any patronizing nonsense about His being a great human teacher. He has not left that open to us. He did not intend to.[1]

---

[1]  Lewis, C.S., *Mere Christianity* (New York: Macmillan, 1952), 56.

# DIVE DEEPER
## Bible and *Catechism* Connections

*Many have committed sin for a trifle.*

—*Sirach 27:1*

*Venial sin weakens charity; it manifests a disordered affection for created goods; it impedes the soul's progress in the exercise of the virtues and the practice of the moral good; it merits temporal punishment. Deliberate and unrepented venial sin disposes us little by little to commit mortal sin.*

—*CCC 1863*

# FIND IT

1. How does Edmund describe the White Witch?

2. Why is the White Witch concerned that Edmund has one brother and two sisters?

3. How is the White Witch's two-fold temptation of Edmund—food and power—similar to the three-fold temptation of Christ?

4. How did the serpent trick Eve in the Garden of Eden?

5. How does the Professor know so much about Narnia?

# TALK IT OUT

1. Although she was evil, the White Witch appeared beautiful to Edmund. Discuss ways or examples in which the devil tries to tempt us by making evil look attractive or beautiful. What does sin really look like?

2. The *Catechism* tells us that venial sins dispose us, little by little, to commit mortal sins. How does giving into a small temptation

lead us to commit bigger and more serious sins? What are some examples of this? What does this tell us about the importance of avoiding venial sins? (Note: A venial sin is a small sin that damages our relationship with God. A mortal sin is a serious sin that completely separates us from God because it concerns a grave or serious matter and is committed with full knowledge and complete consent.)

3. After hearing about Lucy's claim that she had visited another world in the wardrobe, the Professor tells Peter and Susan that there are only three possibilities: Lucy is lying, she is crazy, or she is telling the truth. Since Lucy had always been honest and wasn't crazy, then she must be telling the truth. Would you have believed Lucy? Why or why not? How do these three possibilities relate to Jesus' claim that he was the Son of God? In addition to Jesus' own claim that he was the Son of God, what other evidence is there that he truly was the Son of God. (Hint: Answers might include his many miracles and eyewitness accounts of his resurrection.)

## ACTIVITY
### Write a Proverb

Little by little, Edmund's bad choices led him to make even worse choices. This can be described by this saying: One wrong step on a slippery slope can cause you to slide all the way down.

A proverb is a short saying that reveals truth or gives good advice. Write a proverb that shows the danger of making small mistakes or committing small sins and how they lead to larger sins. Write another proverb showing the virtue in performing small deeds out of love and how that leads to greater acts of love.

# ACTIVITY
## Write a Note

After Edmund is transported to Narnia, he meets the White Witch, who appears to be proud, cold, and stern, and he is afraid of her at first. But later, she begins to speak more kindly and offers him his favorite candy—Turkish Delight. Edmund takes the Turkish Delight and soon finds himself wanting more, which she refuses to give him. However, she promises to give him more if he brings his brother and sisters to meet her.

When you meet someone and a voice inside tells you not to trust them, what might that mean? (Remember that conscience is the interior voice that tells us right from wrong.) Write a note to Edmund advising him why he should follow his conscience and not take the candy. Tell him what it will do to him. Try to convince him that he should not bring his brother and sisters to meet the White Witch and should not go back himself.

# FOR FURTHER EXPLORATION

The Bible contains many eyewitness accounts of Jesus' teachings, his miracles, and his resurrection. However, there are also some historical accounts of Jesus written by people who were not his followers. For example, the Jewish historian Flavius Josephus wrote about Jesus in the year AD 93. The Roman senator Tacitus, the Roman governor Pliny, and the Roman historian Suetonius also mention Jesus. Although they were not believers or followers of Christ, their writings give evidence of the existence of Jesus and what early Christians believed about him. Research what Flavius Josephus, or others, wrote about Jesus. What do they say about the existence of Jesus and the beliefs of early Christians?

# CHAPTER 5

# Once All Four Children Have Entered Narnia

### 37) What effect does sin and selfishness have on Edmund?

Time and time again, Edmund is shown the truth but fails to accept it. When Lucy tells him that a mean witch has caused it to be winter in Narnia (and banished the joyful celebration of Christmas), Edmund tries to convince her that maybe Mr. Tumnus is on the wrong side and that the Witch really is the true Queen of Narnia. Once all four children enter Narnia, Edmund pretends that he has never been there. But he is caught in his lie when he mentions going toward the lamp-post, and he gets angry with Peter for putting Lucy in charge. The lesson here is that selfishness and sin traps Edmund into denying the truth that lies right before his eyes. Sin leads to deeper sin.

### 38) Isn't Edmund like Judas, the apostle who betrayed Jesus?

It seems Edmund's actions are very similar to Judas' betrayal of Jesus. In the New Testament, we see that Judas thinks only of himself and what he will get in return for turning Jesus over to the authorities—thirty silver coins. We are told that, as keeper of the apostles' funds, he was greedy and often took some of the money for his own use (see John 12:6).

Like Judas, Edmund knows deep in his heart that betraying the others is wrong. But the thought of being king and the promise of more Turkish Delight seems to make his actions worthwhile. When Edmund denies to Peter and Susan that he has been to Narnia, he is thinking only of himself and his own selfish desires. He does this to trick them, so that when all four of them enter Narnia, they will follow him to the Witch's castle so he can have more Turkish Delight and be made king.

Neither Judas nor Edmund thinks of the long-term consequences of their actions or of whom they may hurt. They convince themselves that their own needs are more important than those of others. Sin has blinded them to the truth.

### 39) How is Mr. Tumnus' behavior Christ-like?

When Mr. Tumnus meets Lucy and realizes that his service to the Witch is wrong, he is willing to sacrifice his own life for Lucy to do the right thing. Lucy knows he had put his life on the line for her, and she in turn wants to help him in any way she can and to save him from the Witch's evil plans. As members of the Church, the body of Christ, we are called to love our neighbor as ourselves.

### 40) The children know that they should help rescue Mr. Tumnus from the hands of the Witch. Why do they believe this?

The four children know they must help Mr. Tumnus since he helped save Lucy and got her home safely. He helped their sister, and now he needs their help. Our Christian faith teaches us that we are to help all people in need because all are our brothers and sisters. We are called to do good to others and offer our help to those in need regardless of whether it is inconvenient, uncomfortable, or even dangerous to ourselves.

### 41) All four children have a strong emotional reaction to hearing the name Aslan for the first time. Why is this?

As we are told in the story, when the children hear Mr. Beaver speak Aslan's name, "each of [them] felt something jump on the inside." Each experiences something slightly different: Peter feels brave; Susan, a sensation of a "delicious smell" or "delightful music"; and Lucy has a feeling like the "beginning of the holidays" or summer. On some deep level, they perceive that Aslan (whom they've never met nor know anything about at that point) will set things right in Narnia.

Edmund, though, by putting himself at the service of the White Witch, has sided with evil. Since Aslan is the personification of all that is good and true, Edmund, as a result of his sin, feels uneasy and a little afraid at the mention of Aslan. The conflict shows on his face: He knows he is choosing evil, but he remains determined to serve his own desires.

### 42) Who is Aslan?

Aslan is "the Lion, the great Lion." He is majestic in appearance, and his presence inspires awe, devotion, joy, and fear all at the same time. "He isn't safe. But he's good." He is the Creator of Narnia, who sang the world into being in the depths of time (as we learn in *The Magician's Nephew*), and he is likewise the one who will undo the Deep Magic from the Dawn of Time (which requires that blood be shed for sin committed) by the sacrifice of himself (which will cause the even Deeper Magic from Before the Dawn of Time to make death work backward). Those who reject what is good and embrace what is evil are filled with awe, deep hostility, and dread at his presence.

As ruler of Narnia and son of its God, Aslan has to be an animal rather than a human being because Narnia is populated by non-human creatures. He is portrayed as a lion because the lion is the King of the Beasts.

### 43) What are some of Aslan's titles?

Aslan is called "King of the wood," "Lord of the whole wood," "King of the Beasts," and "King above all High Kings." He is the "son of the great Emperor-beyond-the-Sea," "the great Lion." Aslan assures Lucy that she will have his continued presence when she gets to know him by his earthly name.

As an Oxford tutor and a scholar, C.S. Lewis chose the name *Aslan* because he knew it is the Turkish word for *lion*. Also, *As* is an old Scandinavian word meaning *god*, which Lewis may have known.

### 44) Who is the Emperor?

The Emperor-beyond-the-Sea (also shortened to just "the Emperor") is Aslan's father, and it is his declaration of the Deep Magic and the Deeper Magic that Aslan is unwilling— in fact, is unable—to contradict since it is the Law that he himself has established.

When Susan asks if there is anything Aslan can do to save Edmund by going against the Deep Magic, he frowns at her and says, "Work against the Emperor's Magic?" Working against the Emperor's Magic would be akin to rebelling against the Emperor himself. Aslan's response to Susan is reminiscent of Jesus' rebuke to St. Peter—"Get behind me, Satan!" (Matthew 16:23)—when Peter suggests he not undergo his passion and death. It also recalls Jesus' words about the Law of Moses: "Do not think that I have come to abolish the law and the prophets; I have come not to abolish them but to fulfill them" (Matthew 5:17). The Emperor represents God the Father.

### 45) What does the White Witch mean by calling herself Empress?

By assuming the title "Empress," the Witch intends to focus all her powers on conquering Aslan, assuming his place and making herself equal to the Emperor. In her pride, she has deluded herself into believing she can defeat Aslan and continue her terrifying reign over Narnia.

In a similar way, Satan and the other fallen angels (or "demons") sinned in their pride by rebelling against God. As a result, they were cast out of heaven and now seek to tempt us to join their rebellion against God by leading us to sin. We must always strive to live in God's grace by following his teachings in the Bible and the Church, by receiving the sacraments, and by praying that his will be done in our lives.

### 46) Why is the White Witch evil?

Her selfish desires and her lust for power have blinded her to the good. In *The Magician's Nephew*, we learn that she chose to eat the forbidden apple, thus confirming her in her course of rebellion against the Emperor and his son, Aslan. She is determined to do away with the four children because Narnian prophecy states that four humans will sit on the four thrones of Cair Paravel and rule over Narnia. Having seared her conscience in her pride, she will do anything to accomplish her ends. Ultimately, she is destroyed by her own evil deeds.

### 47) Why does the White Witch hate Aslan so much?

Because she has fully embraced evil, she cannot stand to be in the presence of good. She is a slave to what Lewis calls "the Great Sin"—namely, the sin of pride. As he says in *Mere Christianity*, "It was through Pride that the devil became the devil: Pride leads to every other vice: it is the complete anti-God state of mind."[2]

---

[2]   Lewis, C.S., *Mere Christianity* (New York: Macmillan, 1952), 109.

Aslan represents all that is good, true, and holy—he is Goodness itself and Love itself. Pride, by contrast, is enmity, as Lewis points out in *Mere Christianity*:

> Pride is essentially competitive—is competitive by its very nature—while the other vices are competitive only, so to speak, by accident. Pride gets no pleasure out of having something, only out of having more of it than the next man. We say that people are proud of being rich, or clever, or good-looking, but they are not. They are proud of being richer, or cleverer, or better-looking than others. If everyone else became equally rich, or clever, or good-looking there would be nothing to be proud about. It is the comparison that makes you proud: the pleasure of being above the rest. Once the element of competition has gone, pride has gone. That is why I say that Pride is essentially competitive in a way the other vices are not.[3]

So it is understandable that she would hate Aslan and all he stands for. He is a threat to her own power and ambition.

We can see this in our own experience. People who are enmeshed in a life of sin often feel uneasy in the presence of holy men and women. Since they are far from the good, they perceive the holy as a burden, and even hearing others speak about God, Jesus, or the teachings of the Church is difficult for them to bear.

---

[3]  Ibid.

# DIVE DEEPER
## Bible and *Catechism* Connections

*God has highly exalted him and bestowed on him the name which
is above every name, that at the name of Jesus every knee should
bow, in heaven and on earth and under the earth, and every tongue
confess that Jesus Christ is Lord, to the glory of God the Father.*
**—Philippians 2:9-11**

*The invocation of the holy name of Jesus is the simplest way of praying
always. When the holy name is repeated often by a humbly attentive
heart, the prayer is not lost by heaping up empty phrases (cf. Mt 6:7),
but holds fast to the word and "brings forth fruit with patience"
(cf. Lk 8:15). This prayer is possible "at all times" because it is not
one occupation among others but the only occupation: that of loving
God, which animates and transfigures every action in Christ Jesus.*
**—CCC 2668**

# FIND IT

1. Once he has eaten the Turkish Delight, how do Edmund's bad choices begin to multiply? Be specific in your examples.

2. What biblical character is Edmund most similar to at this point in the story? List some of the similarities.

3. Explain how Mr. Tumnus' actions exhibit the second greatest commandment, to love our neighbor as ourselves?

4. In what way is Aslan like God the Father? In what way is he like God the Son?

5. Why is the White Witch so determined to do away with the four children?

# TALK IT OUT

1. When hearing the name of Aslan for the first time, Peter, Susan, and Lucy have a very different reaction than Edmund. Why do you think Edmund had such a different reaction? How might people have different reactions to the Church, the Catholic Faith, the pope, or the saints depending on their relationship with God?

2. Satan rebelled against God and was cast out of heaven. He now tries to get us to disobey God by tempting us to sin. What are some of the things that God has given us to resist this temptation?

3. According to C.S. Lewis, pride is the "Great Sin." How does pride lead us to other sins? What is the opposite of pride, and how does that lead us to practice virtue?

# ACTIVITY

### Holy Name Poster

Christians have always respected the name of Jesus, and devotions to the Holy Name of Jesus have been practiced in the Church for many centuries. The name of Jesus is spelled *ΙΗΣΟΥΣ* (transliteration: "Ihsous") in Greek. One of the devotions to his Holy Name was to create images of the Holy Name, often using the first three letters (IHS) as a symbol. Make a poster depicting an image of the Holy Name in a manner that would inspire devotion. To see some examples, search for images of "IHS" on the Internet.

# ACTIVITY
## Litany of the Holy Name of Jesus

One of the most popular devotions to the Holy Name is to pray the Litany of the Holy Name of Jesus, which can be found on the USCCB website (type "Litany of the Holy Name of Jesus" in the search engine on their main page). It can also be found in many other places online. In praying a litany, one person says the words in the first column, while everyone else says the words in the second column. Make a copy of the litany to pray individually, together, or with your family.

# FOR FURTHER EXPLORATION

C.S. Lewis wrote numerous books throughout his life. Research some of the other books that he wrote. What are some of the different genres or styles he used in his writing? Are there any common themes in the books that he wrote? Is there a book from C.S. Lewis that you would like to read next? Perhaps *Prince Caspian* or another book from *The Chronicles of Narnia* or a different type of book such as *Mere Christianity*?

## CHAPTER 6

# Before Edmund Goes
# to See the Witch

**48) Do all the animals in Narnia talk?**

Remember—Narnia is a magical place. Many of its animals
have an understanding of human language. Some of them,
like Mr. Tumnus and the Beavers, also have the ability to
speak themselves. So, although not all creatures in Narnia
use words, their communication with the children can be
observed (such as when the robin leads them through the
woods to the Beavers by flying from tree to tree).

**49) How many times does Edmund betray his family?**

Three times. The first occasion is when he returns from his
first trip to Narnia through the wardrobe and yet denies to
Susan and Peter that he had been there or even that such a
place exists.

Next, he denies to Peter that the Witch is evil when they are
walking from Mr. Tumnus' home to the Beavers' house. He
tries to trick Peter into thinking that maybe Mr. Beaver is bad

and the Witch is good, and then he asks Peter if he knows the way back home.

Finally, the greatest betrayal of all comes when he learns that the Beavers and his siblings are set to meet Aslan and defeat the Witch. He secretly slips out of the Beavers' home and runs toward the house of the Witch to report everything he has learned. All this he does out of his own selfish desires, that is, for more Turkish Delight and to be made King.

These three acts of betrayal may recall for us the three denials of Christ by St. Peter (see Matthew 26:69-75).

## 50) At what point is there no turning back for Edmund?

This can be seen during Edmund's "betrayal walk" from the Beavers' home to the Witch's castle. He expresses his negative feelings toward Aslan and focuses on what the Witch will show him when they meet. His reaction when Mr. Beaver first mentions Aslan shows that he feels uneasy about the course of action he has decided upon. But his deep-rooted selfishness still drives him to follow the path of sin. He keeps letting himself be tricked by temptation; he tells himself that Peter drove him into leaving, helping him believe he is doing the right thing by going to the Witch.

## 51) Why does Edmund run away from his siblings and the Beavers?

Edmund wants to get to the Witch's house as soon as possible so he could have more Turkish Delight and be made King of Narnia. This is despite the fact that doing so will likely end up hurting his siblings and himself as well.

The true nature of sin is that it harms the person who commits it as well as everyone around them. God does not forbid certain actions to spoil our fun and make our lives difficult. Rather, since he truly loves us and wants what is best for us, he forbids certain things because he knows they are harmful to us, being contrary to our nature as human beings, and will only make us unhappy in the end.

## 52) Is it significant that Edmund commits his final betrayal after having supper with his siblings and the Beavers?

Edmund has been trying to plot when he would betray his family and leave the Beavers during their whole journey in Narnia. Similarly, Judas also betrays Jesus and the apostles out of his own selfish desires. He too was looking for the best opportunity to betray his Master. Like Judas at the Last Supper, Edmund betrays his family after their supper with the Beavers.

## 53) Who is Father Christmas? Can you explain the gifts he gives to the children?

Father Christmas is a commonly used British name for Santa Claus or St. Nicholas. As a legendary figure, Father Christmas is associated with the wonderment of the coming of the Messiah. He embodies the joy of giving and is a symbol of hope to the inhabitants of Narnia, who have endured one hundred dreary years of winter without ever celebrating Christmas.

Instead of giving the children the usual Christmas toys, he gives them practical gifts that will help them during their time in Narnia. They are "survival gifts" to help achieve what they are seeking. Here, Father Christmas seems to be acting as an agent of Aslan (and, by extension, of the Emperor), just as saints do. Interestingly, the gifts he gives are not only useful but reflect something of the true nature of those who receive them. They show something of who Peter, Susan, and Lucy truly are.

Similarly, in prayer and in sacraments such as Baptism and Confirmation, we receive the gift of God's grace to guide and strengthen us to do his will. Like the children in our story, God gives to each of us exactly what we need to carry out his purpose for our lives. When we carry out his will, Jesus reveals not only God to man, but man to himself.

## 54) What specifically does Father Christmas give each of the children and why?

To Peter, the oldest, he gives a sword and a shield and tells him that he will use them soon. The shield has a red lion on it, symbolizing that blood will be shed and that Peter will fight for Aslan and his army. Both the sword and the shield are just the right size and weight; they fit him perfectly, and they will be used well.

To Susan, he gives a bow, a quiver of arrows, and an ivory horn. He tells her that the bow won't easily miss and that the horn, when blown, will bring help in times of danger. When the Wolf attacks, the horn lets Aslan and Peter know that Susan and the others are in danger.

To Lucy, he gives a little bottle containing the juice of the fire flowers that grow on the mountains of the sun. A drop of this liquid is able to heal anyone who is injured or ill. Father Christmas also gives her a small dagger to defend herself in times of great need.

# DIVE DEEPER
### Bible and *Catechism* Connections

*And the Spirit of the LORD shall rest upon him, the spirit
of wisdom and understanding, the spirit of counsel and
might, the spirit of knowledge and the fear of the LORD.*
                                                        **—Isaiah 11:2**

*The seven gifts of the Holy Spirit are wisdom, understanding,
counsel, fortitude, knowledge, piety, and fear of the Lord. They
belong in their fullness to Christ, Son of David (cf. Isa 11:1-2). They
complete and perfect the virtues of those who receive them. They
make the faithful docile in readily obeying divine inspirations.*
                                                        **—CCC 1831**

# FIND IT

1. How were the actions of Edmund, who slipped out of dinner early to go see the White Witch, like those of Judas at the Last Supper?

2. Father Christmas is based on what historical figure in the Catholic Church?

3. In Christianity, the arrival of Father Christmas or Santa Claus is associated with the Birth of Jesus at Christmas. What is the significance of Father Christmas' arrival in Narnia?

4. What gifts does Father Christmas give to Peter, Susan, and Lucy?

5. What do these gifts tell us about the person who received them?

# TALK IT OUT

1. Sin not only harms ourselves but also harms our relationship with God and with other people. However, we sometimes try to tell ourselves that a particular sin isn't really bad because no one is getting hurt. What are some examples of how every sin hurts our relationship with God and other people in some way (e.g., a "white" lie, stealing something of small value, gossiping, saying a "bad" word, and so on)?

2. Writers of fantasy books ask readers to accept things that aren't real. For example, in *The Chronicles of Narnia*, we have talking animals and characters from Roman and Greek mythology. Why do you think C.S. Lewis introduced the character of Father Christmas? Does he seem somewhat out of place when compared to the other characters? What does his presence add to the story?

3. Father Christmas gives Peter, Susan, and Lucy gifts that they will need to accomplish their mission. What gifts does God give us to achieve the mission he has given us as Christians? (Hint: the gifts of the Holy Spirit.)

# ACTIVITY

### Gifts of the Holy Spirit Poster

The seven gifts of the Holy Spirit help us in the mission that we receive in Confirmation, which is to be witnesses of Christ. In your own words, explain how each of these seven gifts help us in the Christian life: wisdom, understanding, counsel (right judgement), fortitude (courage), knowledge, piety (reverence), and fear of the Lord (wonder and awe). Make a poster depicting the Holy Spirit bestowing these seven gifts.

# ACTIVITY

## The Spiritual Significance of the Gifts from Father Christmas

Father Christmas gives Peter a sword and a shield, Susan a bow and arrows and a horn, and Lucy a vial of healing liquid. Peter, Susan, and Lucy use each of these gifts in the mission that they were given in Narnia. Look up the verses below to find the spiritual significance of these gifts in the Bible.

**SWORD** – *Ephesians 6:17; Hebrews 4:12*

**SHIELD** – *Ephesians 6:16; Psalm 18:2*

**ARROWS** – *Psalm 45:5*

**HORN** – *Psalm 18:2; Luke 1:69*

**HEALING CORDIAL/ANOINTING** – *James 5:14*

# FOR FURTHER EXPLORATION

Edmund betrays his family three times. How many times does Peter deny Christ (see Matthew 26:69-75)? And, following his resurrection, how many times does Christ ask Peter if he loves him (see John 21:15-17)? Research the biblical significance of the number three. List several examples from the Bible or Christian teaching that use the number three. For example, there are three Persons in the Blessed Trinity. In what parts of the Mass are words or phrases repeated three times? What is the significance of other numbers commonly found in Scripture, such as six, seven, eight, twelve, and forty.

# CHAPTER 7

# The Children Meet Aslan

**55) Isn't it sometimes difficult to turn away from our sins? How is this seen with Edmund?**

Yes, it is not always easy to leave our sins behind and walk the path of virtue. We can see this in Narnia when Edmund finally realizes that the Witch is truly evil and that she does not really care about his well-being. The path he travels to this realization, though, is a rough one: He is cold as they travel to the Stone Table; he is hit by the Witch when he tries to defend the fox and the others who were having a party in the forest; the Witch orders her servant to tie his arms and pull him along as they travel rapidly through the forest (he keeps falling and has trouble keeping up); and he would have lost his life if Aslan's army had not come to his rescue.

**56) What season follows winter in Narnia? What is significant about this season?**

The darkness and cold of the never-ending winter finally turn into the light and warmth of spring, the season of new life, of resurrection. The arrival of spring—coinciding with the arrival of Aslan—signals the end of the Witch's treacherous reign and heralds a new beginning for the inhabitants of Narnia.

### 57) What are the differences between the reindeer that pulled the sledge (or sleigh) of Father Christmas and those that pulled the sleigh of the White Witch?

For nearly two centuries, and certainly at the time that C.S. Lewis wrote *The Chronicles of Narnia*, Father Christmas has been depicted as arriving on a sleigh with jingling bells pulled by large, brown reindeer. In comparison, the reindeer used by the White Witch were much smaller, about the size of Shetland ponies, and were white, like the White Witch. In the world of Narnia, the color white represents the evil reign of the White Witch, the endless winter, and the absence of new life, joy, happiness, and peace. It also seems appropriate that the antagonist of the Narnian story mirror, albeit in a deficient manner, the traditional depictions of Father Christmas, whose presence in the story portends (or foreshadows) the arrival of Christmas, Aslan, spring, and, most importantly, the end of the reign of the White Witch herself.

### 58) In Narnia, some animals and creatures are good while others are bad because they are allied with the White Witch. Who are the Witch's allies?

The White Witch calls many creatures to do battle against Aslan, including:

- Giants
- Werewolves
- The spirits of evil trees and poisonous plants
- The people of the toadstools

- Boggles (small, grotesque supernatural creatures that make trouble for humans; can evoke feelings of dread and apprehension; also known as hobgoblins or bogeys)

- Ogres (in fairy tales and legends, ugly giants that eat human beings)

- Minotaurs (in Greek mythology, the Minotaur is a monster that had the head of a bull and the body of a man; killed young men and women who were sacrificed to him in the labyrinth where he lived on the island of Crete)

- Incubuses (in Western medieval legend, demons that assault people while they are sleeping; from the Latin *incubare*, "to lie upon")

- Spectres (phantoms, apparitions, or ghosts)

- Wraiths (apparitions of a person who is still alive, seen as a sign or omen that the person is about to die; also used as another word for "ghosts")

- Efreets (powerful evil spirits or, in Arabic mythology, gigantic and monstrous demons)

- Ettins (an ancient name for a giants; originally meant "gluttonous"—i.e., one who eats too much—a disposition that tends to make one large)

## 59) Why does the Wolf deserve a name and title?

Most Narnian creatures are referred to by their animal names only. But the particular wolf that guards the entrance to the Witch's castle and does her deadly bidding is called *Maugrim* (or *Fenris Ulf* in older American editions of the book). He holds the title "Captain of the Secret Police."

Why does the author give such special attention to him? One reason is that all the Narnian animals are placed according to the human traits given them in fairy tales, myths, and legends. In such stories, wolves are typically portrayed as being treacherous, vicious, spiteful, and totally lacking in mercy (see *Aesop's Fables*). Given this, we can see why C.S. Lewis would assign him to the task of being the right-hand "man" to the Witch; he has the perfect temperament to carry out her evil designs.

In his works, Lewis uses imagery from twentieth-century totalitarian governments. We don't normally hear of the "secret police" in old fairy tales. But Lewis thought that for all its many shortcomings in terms of living up to the Gospel, the twentieth century had excelled at one thing: It showed us better than any other age what hell was like. Accordingly, he introduces *The Screwtape Letters* by remarking the following:

[We] live in the Managerial Age, in a world of "Admin." The greatest evil is not now done in those sordid "dens of crime" that Dickens loved to paint. It is not done even in concentration camps and labour camps. In those we see its final result. But it is conceived and ordered (moved, seconded, carried and minuted) in clean, carpeted, warmed, and well-lighted offices, by quiet men with white collars and cut fingernails and smooth-shaven cheeks who do not need to raise their voice. Hence naturally enough, my symbol for Hell is something like the bureaucracy of a police state or the offices of a thoroughly nasty business concern.[4]

We can see something like Screwtape's hellish police state present in the regime of the Witch.

## 60) Which Narnian creatures are on Aslan's side?

When the children first meet Aslan, he is accompanied by naiads, dryads, centaurs, a unicorn, a bull, a pelican, an eagle, a great dog, and two leopards. All these creatures come from Greek mythology and medieval heraldry. Many of them symbolize various virtues—the unicorn symbolizes purity; the pelican, sacrificial love; the eagle, vision; the dog, fidelity; and the leopard, swiftness. Those animals that had been turned to stone by the White Witch and freed from their

---

4    Lewis, C.S., *The Screwtape Letters* (New York: Macmillan, 1961), x.

prisons by the breath of Aslan include dwarfs, horses, giants, lions, other centaurs, unicorns, eagles, and dogs. They join his army and help fight against the forces of the Witch.

### 61) What are *naiads* and *dryads*?

They are female spirit creatures from Greek and Roman mythology. *Naiads* are water nymphs that live in rivers, brooks, springs, and fountains. *Dryads* are wood nymphs that live and die with the trees of which they are the spirits. Their physical appearance reflects the type of tree they live in. Dryads like to dance and are mentioned in *The Chronicles* as the dancing partners of fauns.

In Lewis' world, the figures from pagan mythology who side with Aslan represent the natural human joys and virtues that are meant to find fulfillment in Christ. They also represent nature, submissive in love to the rightful authority of its creator—God. They further image the fact that creation is good, not a merely neutral collection of atoms and energy. As St. Paul says, "The whole creation has been groaning with labor pains together until now" awaiting the day when "creation itself will be set free from its bondage to decay and obtain the glorious liberty of the children of God" (Romans 8:21-22).

### 62) When scuffling over who will approach Aslan first, why does Mr. Beaver say to Peter, "Sons of Adam before animals"?

Mr. Beaver realizes that humans rank higher than animals. His expression is akin to saying "women and children first" in a disaster. According to Narnian prophecy, four humans would come into the land and break the power of the White Witch. They would rule over Narnia with justice from four thrones in Cair Paravel. So the Beaver understands it is far more important to save the children from the Witch than it is to save himself or his family. In addition, by saying "Sons of Adam before animals," he is instructing Peter and the other children of their importance to the future of Narnia. This is reflective of the teaching of Genesis 1 and 2 that human beings, made in the image and likeness of God, have dominion over creation and over the creatures of the earth.

**63)  Explain the discussion between the Witch and her dwarf about the four thrones at Cair Paravel.**

While they were holding Edmund captive, the Witch and the dwarf figure that if only three of the thrones are filled, the prophecy would not be fulfilled and the Witch would not lose her life. While the dwarf recommends they keep Edmund alive as a bargaining chip with Aslan, the Witch recognizes that there is a great danger he would be rescued. Thus they decide to kill him immediately.

**64)  Why does the Witch say the Stone Table is the proper place to kill Edmund?**

The mysterious, deeply carved inscription on the Stone Table calls for the sacrifice of traitors. Since Edmund is clearly a traitor to Aslan and his siblings, the Witch rightly believes that the Stone Table would be the proper place for his death. The Stone Table represents, in part, the Law. Lewis has in mind here both the natural law that enlightens human conscience and the revealed Law of Moses. We know this because Lewis speaks of the Law written on the Table in ways that link it not only to the Emperor's scepter (symbolizing revealed truth) but also with the "World Ash Tree" (an image borrowed from pagan Norse mythology). His point is that the moral law is knowable to all, not just to Jews and Christians. It speaks with unbreakable authority, saying certain things are wrong and must be punished, just as certain things are right and must be rewarded. The Law is unbreakable. Even Aslan himself cannot break it without causing Narnia to be overturned and perish in fire and water.

## 65) When does Edmund realize he is going to be killed?

When Edmund is exhausted from the night ride and long walk, he realizes that the Witch intends to kill him only when she and the dwarf settle on his fate and the dwarf ties him to a tree.

## 66) How is Edmund rescued?

Just as the dwarf is about to cut Edmund's throat, the Witch and the dwarf are attacked by centaurs, unicorns, deer, and birds. The Witch immediately turns herself into a boulder and the dwarf into an old tree stump. Disguised, they escape notice. Their attackers, having rescued Edmund, soon leave.

## 67) Why does Peter receive the title "Sir Peter Wolf's-Bane"?

The word *bane* means to be the cause of fatal injury or ruin, so Peter is recognized as the Wolf's worst enemy when he kills Maugrim in battle.

## 68) How does Aslan treat Edmund upon his safe return to Aslan and his army?

Much like Jesus would have done, Aslan takes Edmund aside and speaks with him privately for a while. He realizes Edmund is truly sorry for his betrayal and is willing to set things right. Aslan even tells Peter, Susan, and Lucy not to talk about it with him. He says this not because it should be forgotten, but because he has forgiven him and Edmund is truly sorry.

## 69) Please explain how Edmund is forgiven.

Lewis repeatedly stresses the significance of forgiveness and the effect it has on both the person who is asking for forgiveness and the person being forgiven. Mr. Tumnus, after trying to trick Lucy into falling asleep in his home, asks if she can forgive him, and she does so willingly and lovingly. At the beginning, you see the hurt it causes Lucy when Edmund asks for forgiveness about not believing in Narnia and then turns his back and lies to Susan and Peter about it. Later, Peter asks for Lucy's forgiveness when he finds out that Narnia does in fact exist. Then Aslan forgives Edmund for his ultimate betrayal and so do his siblings, which helps bring Edmund back to his old self again and renews his ties with his family. Here Lewis is clearly trying to show that Jesus teaches us that asking for forgiveness when we are truly sorry and forgiving those who are sorry are the right things to do. In fact, he tells us that if we will not forgive others, we shall not be forgiven (see Mark 11:25).

## DIVE DEEPER

### Bible and *Catechism* Connections

*The wages of sin is death, but the free gift of God
is eternal life in Christ Jesus our Lord.*

—**Romans 6:23**

*Jesus invites sinners ... to that conversion without which one cannot
enter the kingdom, but shows them in word and deed his Father's
boundless mercy for them. ... The supreme proof of his love will be
the sacrifice of his own life "for the forgiveness of sins" (Mt 26:28).*

—*CCC 545*

## FIND IT

1. What is the significance of spring in Narnia? What is its significance in Christianity?

2. According to C.S. Lewis, at what did the twentieth century excel?

3. What do the mythological characters who side with Aslan represent?

4. What is the significance of Mr. Beaver saying, "Sons of Adam before animals"?

5. What is the purpose of the Stone Table? And why is it appropriate that Edmund be killed there?

## TALK IT OUT

1. In Genesis 1, God created man and woman in his image and likeness and gave them dominion over all of creation. What is the significance of this, and what implications does it have in regard to how we are to treat the natural world?

2. The "law" of Narnia calls for traitors to be sacrificed at the Stone Table, and not even Aslan can break the law. Likewise, Scripture tells us that "the wages of sin is death" (Romans 6:23). Why did Jesus have to die for our sins instead of just saying that everyone was forgiven?

3. Following his rescue, Edmund tells Aslan that he is sorry for his betrayal, and Aslan forgives him, telling the others not to speak to Edmund about his actions again. What does this teach us about God's forgiveness, and how we should forgive others?

## ACTIVITY
### Role Play

Edmund said that he was sorry for his betrayal, first to Aslan and then to his brother and sisters. Role-play a scene in which someone expresses sorrow for what he or she has done wrong and how those actions have hurt others. The others should forgive that person and welcome him or her back into their friendship. When finished, the role-play can continue with another person playing the part of the wrongdoer.

## ACTIVITY

### Make a List

In Genesis 1, we read that God created Adam and Eve in his image and likeness. He blessed them and gave them "dominion over the fish of the sea and over the birds of the air and over every living thing that moves upon the earth" (Genesis 1:28). A steward is a person who takes care of something for its rightful owner. The world belongs to God, so our dominion over the earth is in the form of stewardship. Make a list of practical things that you can do to take better care of the earth, its natural resources, and the animals as a faithful steward of God.

## FOR FURTHER EXPLORATION

While most of the characters in Narnia come from fairy tales, C.S. Lewis introduced some characters from the twentieth century, such as the secret police. At the time that he wrote *The Lion, The Witch and the Wardrobe*, Lewis would have been very aware of the Gestapo, or secret police of the Nazi party, which was one of the most ruthless secret police organizations of the twentieth century. What was their purpose, what were some of their tactics, and why were they such a danger to human freedom? What does this tell us about the White Witch?

CHAPTER 8

# Aslan, the Witch, and Redemption

## 70) Why does Aslan bargain with the Witch?

Aslan offers the Witch a target even more tempting than
Edmund's life—his own. Like Jesus, Aslan puts himself in
a position where (it would seem) the devil can have the
ultimate victory by killing God himself. He offers his life
freely for Edmund's, despite the fact that Edmund, far from
deserving such a sacrifice, is actually worthy of death. The
Witch, in her hatred of Aslan, likewise freely takes the bait in
the hope of destroying Aslan once and for all, and with the
intention of afterward destroying the children as well and
placing all of Narnia forever in her grip.

## 71) What do Aslan and Father Christmas prepare Peter for?

Aslan and Father Christmas prepare Peter for the impending
great battle against the White Witch and her allies. Father
Christmas gives him the sword and shield for fighting, and
Aslan tells him what he must do. Like St. Peter in the Bible, to

whom Jesus gives authority to lead the apostles (see Matthew 16:18-19), he must use the tools Father Christmas and Aslan have given him if he is to fulfill his destiny.

## 72)  Is there any significance to Peter's name?

His name is from a Greek word meaning "rock," and this shows his strength and character. As the oldest, his siblings look up to him and rely upon him to make the important decisions. Ultimately, Peter is to be the "rock" for not only his brother and sisters but also all of Narnia as well.

After killing the Wolf and fighting with Aslan's forces in the Great Battle against the Witch, he is eventually crowned High King. Similar to the apostle Peter, he plays an important role in leading the "good army" to victory, and it is he whom Aslan talks to the most about leading his people. Similarly, he reigns with another king and two queens as the "first among equals," just as St. Peter was the chief of the apostles yet the servant of all.

## 73)  When Aslan tells Peter he may not be there physically with him for the battle so Peter must listen and act, what is Aslan trying to do?

He wants Peter to be prepared and to know that with Aslan's guidance he can fight physically by himself because Aslan is with him. Jesus equips us with what we need too, and we must trust him, like Peter must trust Aslan. Jesus may not be with us physically as he was with his apostles, but he is always with us. After he rose to heaven in front of the twelve apostles, although he was not with them physically, he remained with them by sending the Holy Spirit. He calls us to act in obedience to him in order to grow in grace and in the strength of the Holy Spirit. So, as St. Paul tells us in Philippians 2:12-13, "Work out your own salvation with fear and trembling" (which, as Lewis observed, makes it sound as though *we* are to do everything) "for God is at work in you, both to will and to work for his good pleasure" (which, as Lewis also observed, makes it sound as though *God* is doing everything). So Peter acts freely, using all the gifts Aslan has given him. It is he who wins the battle, yet it is only by Aslan's power that he does so.

### 74) Why can the White Witch not look directly into Aslan's eyes?

The White Witch knows Aslan is more powerful than she, but she cannot resist confronting and trying to conquer him. She deludes herself into thinking that she just needs to figure out how. The Witch, having committed herself to evil, cannot endure being in the presence of good. Evil, a parasite upon good and dependent on it for existence, can never bear to face true Goodness.

### 75) What does Aslan mean by "his offense was not against you," when speaking to the Witch about Edmund?

Throughout the story, Edmund is serving his pride and gluttony. He repeatedly and deliberately chooses to do anything necessary—however evil—to satisfy his desires. It is not that he chooses to ally himself with the Witch for her sake. Rather, he only wants what she promises to give him.

Most people don't sin because they deliberately seek to align themselves with evil. Rather, they allow themselves to fall into sin because of some "good" they want—power, pleasure, money, and so on. As fallen human beings, we can easily delude ourselves into thinking something bad is really good simply to satisfy our own desires. If anything, Edmund has sought to serve the Witch, not harm her. Aslan's point is that her claim on Edmund's life is, like everything else, rooted in a lie. She herself has tempted him to be a traitor. She therefore has a claim on his blood, but it is a lie that his offense is against her. In truth, he has offended Aslan, who is willing to offer his life for Edmund nonetheless.

### 76) How can Edmund be unaware of the Witch's presence when she and Aslan meet?

Although no one hears Aslan's talk with Edmund, it is remarkable how after their walk, Edmund keeps his gaze directed upon Aslan. By resting his eyes only on the Lion, we can see that he has freely and without reservation chosen to follow the Good. By not even giving evil (in the form of the Witch) a glance, Edmund appears to have had a true conversion experience. He will probably not allow himself to be drawn into sin again. His goal is not to fight the evil of the Witch with his own strength (which is simply another form of pride) but to love Aslan and trust him.

As Christians, we commit ourselves to following God's will in our lives. As such, we should pay no attention to the temptations the devil throws our way; we should always keep our eyes fixed on God and his loving plan.

### 77) What is the Stone Table?

The Stone Table is a large slab of grey stone, supported by four upright pillars of stone. As we have already seen, it partly symbolizes the moral law. But there is more to the Stone Table. For it is also a place upon which sacrifice is made. The White Witch states that the Stone Table is the proper place for killing and the place where killing has always been done.

Although its size is not mentioned in the book, the Stone Table would need to be low in height because the two girls are able to kneel and still kiss Aslan's face as he lies on top of it. Unknown to the White Witch, it was decreed before the beginning of time that the Table would crack when an innocent victim was willingly killed in the place of a traitor and that death would work backward. This is exactly the circumstances of Aslan's self-sacrifice on behalf of Edmund. As soon as the sun comes up in Narnia following the death of Aslan, the Table immediately breaks in half with a loud noise and the Risen Lion appears to the girls.

## 78) What does the Stone Table represent?

We can see that the Stone Table closely resembles an altar.
In the Old Testament, God commanded his chosen people,
the Israelites, to offer him animal sacrifices on an altar in
atonement for their sins. The Church has celebrated the Holy
Eucharist on an altar from the very beginning. Our Catholic
Faith teaches that the Eucharist is the *re-presentation* of the
sacrifice of Jesus on the Cross and that the bread and wine
truly become the Body and Blood of Christ.

## 79) Why does the Witch claim Edmund belongs to her?

The Witch maintains that the inscription on the Stone Table
(the Deep Magic) makes Edmund hers because he is a traitor.
As she says, "His life is forfeit to me. His blood is my property."
She explains her rights according to the Deep Magic. "[Aslan]
knows that unless I have blood as the Law says all Narnia will
be overturned and perish in fire and water." With these words,
the Witch is merely affirming the order of things as set down
by the Emperor, an order that must be followed or the very
foundation of Narnia would be destroyed.

## 80) What is the Deep Magic?

The Deep Magic is written on the Stone Table and is engraved
on the scepter of the Emperor-beyond-the-Sea. It says that
every traitor belongs to the White Witch as her lawful prey
and that for every treachery she has a right to exact the
ultimate punishment—death.

Here we can see a parallel between the "Deep Magic"
in Narnia and the moral law expressed in the Ten
Commandments of the Old Testament. With the original sin
of Adam and Eve, mankind fell into a state of sin, suffering,
and death. In a sense, we became slaves of the devil—just as
Edmund could be said to be a slave of the White Witch. God,
in his great love and mercy, offers salvation to humanity,
first by putting the natural law into the hearts of all, then by

choosing a people—the Israelites—to whom he reveals his law of life. In this Law, God decrees that his people must offer the sacrifice of animals in atonement for their sins. These sacrifices would last until the ultimate sacrifice for sin, the passion, death, and resurrection of Jesus, would definitively end the reign of sin and bring about the kingdom of God.

### 81) What is "the Magic that is deeper than the Deep Magic"?

We are told that the Deep Magic traces only to the dawn of time. A little further back, though, before time dawned, there was a different incantation: the "Deeper Magic." This decree of the Emperor states that when a willing victim who had committed no treachery—i.e., one who is totally innocent—is killed in a traitor's stead, the Stone Table would crack and death itself would start working backward. This incantation was unknown to the White Witch, so she willingly agrees to Aslan's offer of himself in place of Edmund. She mistakenly believes her moment of victory is at hand.

Similarly, the devil undoubtedly rejoiced at the death of Jesus, not fully understanding the full plan of redemption God had decreed. With Jesus' resurrection, though, sin, death, and Satan are defeated.

### 82) After Peter, Susan, and Lucy are brought to meet Aslan, they prepare for a feast celebrating that the four thrones of Cair Paravel will be filled. But we soon read "good times having just begun were already drawing to an end." What does this mean?

As they prepare for the great feast, they experience joy and peace being with Aslan and seeing the happiness he has brought to all Narnia. They know that the power of the White Witch is coming to an end and that spring is about to arrive. They do not fully realize, though, the battle that must be fought—and the sacrifice Aslan must make—before the final victory over the Witch can be achieved.

Here we can see a parallel with the earthly life of Jesus. Right up until his entry into Jerusalem for Passover, things seemed to be going pretty well. These were "good times" for his apostles; they did not yet fully grasp all Jesus needed to suffer, and they probably expected things would only get better. After all, Jesus' popularity led the people of Jerusalem to welcome him with palm branches and shouts of "hosanna" (see Matthew 21:6-11). Known as a prophet powerful in word and deed, many people had heard his word and had come miles to be in his presence. Not a few of his disciples were more or less hoping for this to continue forever. However, very shortly after the Last Supper, Jesus' passion took place.

## 83) Does there seem to be an obvious connection between the Last Supper of Jesus and the great feast with Aslan?

Yes. We can see how the children's feast with Aslan reflects Jesus' Last Supper with his apostles. After sharing a final meal with those who were closest to them, both Jesus and Aslan soon give up their lives and suffer cruel deaths. Both know that they have to sacrifice their lives for the benefit of others.

## 84) What similarities exist between the suffering, death, and resurrection of Aslan and of Jesus?

The similarities are striking. They include the following:

- Both willingly lay down their lives to save others. In Aslan's sacrifice, Edmund is spared and Narnia restored; in Jesus' sacrifice, the whole world is saved from sin and death, and the kingdom of heaven is opened to those who accept Jesus as savior. (See Romans 8:2; 2 Peter 1:10-11)

- Though both know their deaths are necessary, they are sad and afraid. Much like Jesus' agony in the garden, Aslan on his way to his death is in much agony and pain in the forest and asks his friends to stay with him. (See Matthew 26:36-38)

- In their sufferings, both Aslan and Jesus are treated cruelly and unmercifully by their torturers, but neither ever complain, protest, or resist; they willingly accept whatever happens to them. (See Matthew 26:47–27:56)

- Aslan, like Jesus, is careful to make sure that the blow falls on him alone and that his friends are not swept up in the frenzy of his killers and harmed. And, like Jesus, it is women who remain most faithful to Aslan in his darkest hour and beyond. (See Matthew 26:47-56; John 19:25)

- Susan and Lucy watch Aslan's sufferings helplessly, knowing that there is nothing they can do. Similarly, Jesus' mother, Mary, and Mary Magdalene watch him die on Calvary and also know they can do nothing and that it has to be done. (See John 19:25)

- Aslan is mocked and ridiculed during his torment and even endures having a muzzle put on him. This mirrors Jesus' crowning with thorns and the mockery he endured. (See John 19:1-3)

- Once the crowd of tormentors departs, the girls approach Aslan's body, take off the muzzle, and wipe away his blood. Here we see a parallel with Jesus being taken down from the Cross and those who love him removing the crown of thorns and cleansing his body of the blood. (See Luke 23:50-56)

- Eventually the sky turns gold as the sun rises. Then the girls hear a loud noise as the Stone Table splits in two. This is reminiscent of the curtain in the Temple being torn in two at the death of Jesus. When the girls go back to the table where Aslan has been lying, he is not there (much like Jesus' body was not in the tomb when the stone is removed). (See Matthew 27:51; 28:1-10)

- Susan and Lucy believe Aslan is a ghost until he asks them to touch his mane and they feel the warmth of his breath.

This is similar to Jesus' disciples not believing it is him until they see and feel his wounds. (See John 20:24-29)

## 85) So *is* Aslan an allegorical representation of Jesus?

Yes and no. As Narnia scholar Andrew Rislen has stated, "Aslan both is and is not Jesus." According to C.S. Lewis himself, Aslan takes the role of a Christ-like figure, though he is *not* an allegorical portrayal of Christ: "If Aslan represented the immaterial Deity, he would be an allegorical figure. In reality, however, he is an invention giving an imaginary answer to the question, 'What might Christ become like if there really were a world like Narnia and he chose to be incarnate and die and rise again in that world as he actually has done in ours?' This is not allegory at all."

# DIVE DEEPER
### Bible and *Catechism* Connections

*"Whoever would be great among you must be your servant, and whoever would be first among you must be slave of all. For the Son of man also came not to be served but to serve, and to give his life as a ransom for many."*
**—Mark 10:43-45**

*The Scriptures had foretold this divine plan of salvation through the putting to death of "the righteous one, my Servant" as a mystery of universal redemption, that is, as the ransom that would free men from the slavery of sin (Isa 53:11; cf. 53:12; Jn 8:34-36; Acts 3:14).*
**—CCC 601**

# FIND IT

1. In bargaining with the White Witch for the life of Edmund, how is Aslan acting like Christ?

2. What is the biblical significance of the name Peter? What is the significance of Jesus changing Simon's name to Peter?

3. Why does Edmund keep his eyes on Aslan instead of looking at the White Witch?

4. What is the purpose of an altar, and what is the Eucharist?

5. Who is the ultimate sacrifice for sin? What does that sacrifice set us free from?

# TALK IT OUT

1. The author states: "So Peter acts freely, using all the gifts Aslan has given him. It is he who wins the battle, yet it is only by Aslan's power that he does so." Likewise, before Christ ascended into heaven, he gave his disciples a mission and promised them the Holy Spirit (and the gifts of the Holy Spirit) would assist them. Discuss how we must act freely, using the gifts that God gives us, yet it is only by God's power that we can do anything.

2. Most people don't choose evil for the sake of evil but simply fall into sin because of some "good" that they want, such as power, pleasure, or money. What are some examples of choosing to sin, not because we want to do evil, but because we want something that we think will make us happy?

3. Discuss the similarities between what happened to Aslan at the Stone Table and the death and resurrection of Jesus? What are the differences in their stories?

# ACTIVITY
## Writing

As Christians, we know that Jesus rose again three days after his death on the Cross. However, it would have been quite a different experience for the apostles who did not fully understand that he would rise again. Putting yourself in the place of Susan and Lucy, write a short paragraph about how you would have felt as you witnessed the suffering and death of Aslan. What would it have been like to witness him unexpectedly coming back to life again?

# ACTIVITY
## Bible Search

Knowing that he would not be at the Great Battle, at least in the beginning, Aslan prepares Peter to lead his army. Likewise, knowing that he was going to ascend into heaven forty days after his resurrection, Christ gave his disciples instructions and the authority to carry out his mission. Look up the following verses in the Bible and write one sentence for each, explaining what Christ gave to his disciples or instructed them to do: Matthew 28:19; Mark 16:15; Luke 24:13-35; Luke 24:44-48; John 20:22; John 20:23; and John 21:15-19. (Note: Three of these refer to sacraments.) In what ways are each of these things still occurring in the Church today?

# FOR FURTHER EXPLORATION

The Shroud of Turin is a burial shroud—a large rectangular sheet of linen cloth used to cover the body of a deceased person—that depicts the image of a crucified man. While the Catholic Church has made no statement on its authenticity, many believe it to be the burial shroud of Christ that was mentioned in the Bible (see Matthew 27:59 and John 20:6-7). What does the image tell us about the person who was wrapped in the shroud? In what ways does this fit the biblical account of Jesus' suffering and death? You can also view a 3D image online to have a better idea of what the crucified man in the shroud would have looked like.

CHAPTER 9

# After Aslan's Triumph

### 86) Why does the Stone Table crack?

The Stone Table cracks because the conditions are met for "the magic deeper than the Deep Magic." Aslan has sacrificed himself for Edmund, only to rise again to end the reign of the White Witch and bring about peace and justice in Narnia.

Similarly, St. Paul tells us that the law, having brought us to Christ, no longer has power over us. That does not mean that we are now free to break the law, for example, to murder, steal, or covet to our hearts' desire. Rather, it means that the law was like a tutor whose purpose was to bring us to Jesus. Just as grade school is meant to prepare us for high school, and high school for college, and college for a successful career, the law was to prepare us for the guidance of the Holy Spirit, who makes us able to transcend the law, not break it. Living by the law of love in Christ, we fulfill everything the moral law requires.

**87)  Aslan says to Susan and Lucy that the Witch knew part of the mystery of the Stone Table, but there was a "magic deeper that she did not know." What does this mean?**

The Witch, though powerful, is not as powerful as Aslan, who is the creator of Narnia and knowledgeable in the ways of his father, the Emperor. She was not present before the dawn of time and was thus ignorant of the "Deeper Magic." In a similar way, the devil, though powerful as a fallen angel, does not know the mind of God or have a perfect knowledge of his plans.

St. Paul, speaking of both the human and demonic "rulers" who conspired to murder Jesus, declares, "But we impart a secret and hidden wisdom of God, which God decreed before the ages for our glorification. None of the rulers of this age understood this; for if they had, they would not have crucified the Lord of glory" (1 Corinthians 2:7-8).

**88)  How does the Deeper Magic relate to the Eucharist?**

The Deeper Magic is known only to Aslan and his father, the Emperor, and then believed by those who witness its power.

The Eucharist is the most profound miracle God grants us. The sacred consecration of bread and wine becoming the Body and Blood of Christ was instituted by Jesus, and he shared that with his disciples, who then shared this with the rest of God's people. Only those who have a deep faith can really believe, see, and witness the "deeper magic" of the bread and wine becoming the Body and Blood of Jesus.

**89)  Why does Aslan offer himself to be sacrificed?**

Aslan tells the girls that if someone is sacrificed in the place of a sinner, then "the Table would crack and death itself would start working backwards." This is a parallel to Jesus' sacrifice on the Cross so that all sinners can have eternal life.

**90) What is similar about how Aslan and Jesus both return?**

When he comes back to life, Aslan, like Jesus, appears as he was before his brutal torture and death. His broken body is completely healed, and he has the power of immortality about him.

## DIVE DEEPER
### Bible and *Catechism* Connections

*We know that Christ being raised from the dead will never die again; death no longer has dominion over him. ... So you also must consider yourselves dead to sin and alive to God in Christ Jesus.*
—**Romans 6:9-11**

*Incorporated into Christ by Baptism, Christians are "dead to sin and alive to God in Christ Jesus" and so participate in the life of the Risen Lord (Rom 6:11 and cf. 6:5; cf. Col 2:12).*
—**CCC 1694**

## FIND IT

1. What does Aslan coming back to life mean for the White Witch? What does it mean for Narnia?

2. What was the purpose of the Law in the Old Testament? How was it fulfilled?

3. Why did the White Witch not know about the "Deeper Magic"?

4. In Narnia, when someone was sacrificed in place of a sinner, what would happen to the Stone Table and death?

5. What is the most profound miracle that God gives us? What is required to see it?

# TALK IT OUT

1. How are the events surrounding Aslan at the Stone Table similar to Christ's sacrifice on the Cross and his resurrection three days later? How are they different?

2. The White Witch was ignorant of the "Deeper Magic" and, therefore, thought that she had won a great victory by putting Aslan to death. How does this relate to Satan, who thought he had won a great victory when Jesus was crucified?

3. When Aslan comes back to life, his broken body had been healed and his appearance was one of immortality. How is this similar to Jesus' appearance after his resurrection? How is it different? (Hint: See John 20:24-29.)

# ACTIVITY
### Write a Thank-You Card

In Narnia, Aslan, who was completely innocent, died in the place of Edmund, who was guilty of treason. How do you think Edmund would have felt if he knew that Aslan had died in his place? In a similar way, Jesus, who was completely innocent, suffered and died for the sins of every person. How does this make you feel? Grateful, appreciative, greater love for Jesus, sorrow for sin, resolved to avoid sin, desirous to imitate Jesus more closely? Write a thank-you card, thanking Jesus for his sacrifice on the Cross and all that he has done for us.

# ACTIVITY
## Virtual Tour of the Church of the Holy Sepulcher

Take a virtual tour of the Church of the Holy Sepulcher in Jerusalem. (You can find several virtual tours online.) This ancient church is built around the sites of Jesus' crucifixion and burial, and it has been an important pilgrimage site since the fourth century. Just as the broken Stone Table was a symbol of Aslan's victory in Narnia, the empty tomb is a symbol of Christ's victory over sin and death. After taking the virtual tour, discuss any thoughts that you have.

# FOR FURTHER EXPLORATION

In his post-resurrection appearances to his disciples, Jesus bore the marks of his crucifixion (see Luke 24:40 and John 20:27). While everyone is called to imitate Christ in their lives, in a few rare occasions throughout history, such as in the case of St. Padre Pio, Jesus has allowed a person to bear the marks of his crucifixion on his or her own body. This miracle of having the wounds of Christ in one's hands and feet is called the *stigmata*. Research the life of Padre Pio. Why might Christ have given him the privilege and the burden of the *stigmata*?

CHAPTER 10

# The Great Battle

**91)** **What event in *The Lion, the Witch and the Wardrobe* represents the power of the Holy Spirit?**

When Aslan breathes new life into the statues at the Witch's castle, he does what God did when creating Adam—he "breathed into his nostrils the breath of life, and man became a living soul" (Genesis 2:7). He also does what Jesus did in an even more profound way when he breathed on the apostles and said, "Receive the Holy Spirit" (John 20:22).

After Aslan breathes on all the animals, Lewis describes their restoration to life as looking like a flame as it burns a piece of paper. Instead of turning to ash, however, the stone turns into the animal's flesh. This calls to mind not only the "breath" of the Spirit but also the tongues of fire that appeared over the heads of the apostles on Pentecost, the birthday of the Church (see Acts 2:3). The breath of Aslan restores those who were dead to the life. Now that the animals have been restored, Aslan reminds them that their work is not yet finished and that they must find the battle and help defeat the Witch and her army. Similarly, the Christian is called, by his Baptism and Confirmation, to do battle with the world, the flesh, and the devil.

### 92) After this, what does Aslan command that Jesus also constantly commands us to do?

Aslan makes sure that all of the animals take care of each other and use their strength to that end. In short, he commands them to love one another as he has loved them (see John 15:17). He makes sure that those who cannot keep up (the children, dwarfs, and small animals) are riding on those who can run quickly and are strong (centaurs, unicorns, horses, giants, and eagles). Aslan uses the natural talent of the lions and dogs (that is, their smell) to help them locate the battle.

Jesus calls on us to do the same thing. We who are strong and materially blessed have a duty to protect the weak and the poor, those who cannot take care of themselves—the unborn, the disabled, the dying. We are also called to use the gifts God has given us to better the kingdom of God on earth (see 1 Corinthians 12:4-27).

# DIVE DEEPER
### Bible and *Catechism* Connections

*"Peace be with you. As the Father has sent me, even so I send you." And when he had said this, he breathed on them, and said to them, "Receive the Holy Spirit. If you forgive the sins of any, they are forgiven; if you retain the sins of any, they are retained."*

*—John 20:21-23*

*Confirmation is the full outpouring of the Holy Spirit as once granted to the apostles on the day of Pentecost. ... It gives us a special strength of the Holy Spirit to spread and defend the faith by word and action as true witnesses of Christ, to confess the name of Christ boldly, and never to be ashamed of the Cross (cf. Council of Florence [1439]: DS 1319; LG 11; 12).*

*—CCC 1302–1303*

# FIND IT

1. What happens when Aslan breathes on the statues?

2. What are two examples from Scripture when God the Father and God the Son breathed on someone?

3. After he brings them back to life, what does Aslan "command" the animals to do?

4. What does Christ command us to do in John 15:17?

5. In Narnia, after being brought back to life, the animals help in the fight against the White Witch. What is the mission for Christians who have received a strengthening in the Holy Spirit in the sacrament of Confirmation?

# TALK IT OUT

1. C.S. Lewis uses the imagery of fire when he describes Aslan breathing new life into the statues. How does this imagery represent the power of the Holy Spirit? (Hint: See Acts 2:1-4.)

2. In Confirmation, we are given the strength to be soldiers of Christ, and the author states that we are called to do battle against the world, the flesh, and the devil. The world represents human success, wealth, and power, while the flesh represents our own human weakness. What are some ways in which we can be tempted by the world, the flesh, and the devil, and what can we do to overcome these temptations?

3. In Narnia, Aslan instructs the animals to help each other. List ways in which we can follow Christ's command to love our neighbor as ourselves.

# ACTIVITY

## Make a Quiz

Using the Internet, research a saint and write down one well-known fact about that saint, beginning with the word "I." For example, "I founded the Dominican Order," or "I am called the Little Flower." There should be five statements about five different saints. When finished, give your five statements to someone else, who can use the Internet to find the answers. Once everyone has written down their answers, each person should read the statements and the answers aloud.

## ACTIVITY

### Confirmation Names

In preparing to receive the sacrament of Confirmation, confirmands choose a saint for their Confirmation name. They should have a special devotion to the saint, or the saint should have a particular personality, virtue, or story that they would like to imitate in their own lives. Research the life of a saint that you might like to choose for your Confirmation name and write a short paragraph about why you might choose this saint. If you have already been confirmed, write a short paragraph explaining why you chose that particular saint.

## FOR FURTHER EXPLORATION

In Narnia, Aslan "knights" Peter by striking him with the flat edge of the sword. This form of dubbing a knight developed from an earlier medieval practice in which knights were given a (strong) blow or "slap" to the cheek in the knighting ceremony. This was a reminder that they should never forget their oath as a knight. At about the same time in history, Catholic liturgical books instructed that the bishop, after anointing a person with holy chrism in the sacrament of Confirmation, should give them a (very slight) blow or "slap" to the cheek. This was to remind them that they should never forget their responsibilities as a soldier (or witness) of Christ. Research the "Ten Commandments of the Code of Chivalry." In what ways are these rules for knightly conduct still applicable to all Christians today?

CHAPTER 11

# After the Battle

## 93) What is the meaning behind the magical cordial that Father Christmas gives to Lucy?

The cordial Lucy has been given reminds us of the healing and sanctifying power of Baptism. It is supposed to have great healing powers and was given to her by Father Christmas. The cordial is reminiscent of Jesus' words: "Whoever drinks of the water that I shall give him will never thirst; the water that I shall give him will become in him a spring of water welling up to eternal life" (John 4:14).

## 94) Why does Aslan rebuke Lucy?

Aslan rebukes Lucy because she lingers over Edmund when her duty is to help everyone who has been hurt in the battle. Aslan asks, "Must *more* people die for Edmund?" in part to remind her of the suffering he has endured already for Edmund and also to remind her that her responsibility extends beyond her immediate family. The rebuke is stern but loving, for it is aimed at reminding her that she is a queen and that her responsibility is for the whole realm of Narnia. In the same way, Jesus reminds us that we are not simply to love those who love us, nor to care only for our immediate relatives and friends, but that our call is to love our neighbor—that is, anyone we meet.

## 95) Edmund's appearance changes throughout *The Lion, the Witch and the Wardrobe*. Is this connected with his actions?

Yes, this seems to be the case. We can see this at various points in the story. On their way back home after their first adventure together in Narnia, Lucy asks Edmund if he feels OK because he doesn't look well. This is after he has eaten the Turkish Delight and decided to turn his siblings over to the White Witch. He replies, "I am alright," but it seems clear that evil is affecting his appearance. By contrast, at the end of the story, after his talk with Aslan and being healed from the great battle by the special potion Father Christmas gave to Lucy, the others comment on how well he looks again. By being converted to the good, Edmund has healed from his physical wounds and from the evil that he had allowed to overtake him.

Ultimately, it is Aslan's sacrifice of his very life that saves Edmund from the consequences of his sin and restores him to health. Lucy wants to tell Edmund all about what Aslan did for him, but Susan convinces her how awful it would be for him to know. As Christians, we know the total sacrifice that Jesus made for us on the Cross, yet we continue to sin. Out of love for us, Jesus suffered and died in a way that we could not imagine enduring—to save us from our sins and give us eternal life.

### 96) How does Aslan provide food for everyone the day after the battle?

He provides the food through working a miracle. This event bears a striking similarity to Jesus' feeding of the five thousand by multiplying five loaves and two fish (see Mark 6:35-44).

### 97) Why does the White Stag appear at the end of the story?

The White Stag appears at the end of the story to lead the four children—now the four rulers of Narnia—home to our world, but only if they freely choose to follow him.

In a similar way, Jesus is the Good Shepherd who will lead us if we choose to follow him willingly. He became man and died for us so that we would join him in eternal life.

The white stag is a medieval symbol of Christ. In other words, this is another appearance of Aslan "in disguise." It is he who leads the children back to our world because he is, in fact, the Lord of both Narnia and our world. While trying to follow the White Stag, the four children are led back to the lamp-post and wardrobe door, back to their home.

### 98) What symbolism is associated with a stag in European mythology?

The stag is a symbol of Christ. A white stag is also a familiar creature in Celtic and northern European myths and legends. Its appearance is an indicator of the near presence of the "Otherworld." In this case, the White Stag leads the children back to their world.

When all four of them have followed the White Stag to the lamp-post, they don't know that their world and home lie just beyond. None of the four fully remember the lamp-post. They are not aware that the wardrobe—and their old lives—lies right ahead of them.

**99) The Professor says, "I don't think it will be any good trying to go back through the wardrobe door to get the coats. ... You won't get into Narnia again by that route. ... Indeed, don't try to get there at all. It'll happen when you're not looking for it. ... Keep your eyes open." What does he mean by this?**

The very nature of Narnia and its connection with our world makes it impossible to go back to it the same way. In fact, the children should not even seek to go back, as the Professor tells them. Rather, when Narnia needs them, it will call to them and lead them back in.

We cannot force open a door to heaven; we cannot find our own way there. We cannot *make* grace happen by our willpower. We cannot force God's hand or put him in our debt. As Jesus puts it, "You did not choose me. I chose you" (John 15:16). God promises us that he desires us to come to him and to know him. But this must happen according to his will, not ours. We have been given insights as to what heaven is like (for example, in the Holy Eucharist, marriage, and children), but to find the way to heaven, we must keep our eyes on God and live a Christian life. If we do this, God will call us there in his good time.

**100) What happens to Peter, Susan, Edmund, and Lucy when they pass through the wardrobe back into our world?**

They find that, despite the fact that they have lived for years in Narnia and grown to adulthood there, when they return to our world, no time at all has passed and they are again the ages they were when they entered the wardrobe. This recalls the fact that "with the Lord one day is as a thousand years, and a thousand years as one day" (2 Peter 3:8). It also reminds us that children can be far wiser than adults because of their hearts being open to God. As Jesus says, "Truly, I say to you, whoever does not receive the kingdom of God like a child shall not enter it" (Mark 10:15).

# DIVE DEEPER
### Bible and *Catechism* Connections

*"Go therefore and make disciples of all nations, baptizing them in the name of the Father and of the Son and of the Holy Spirit, teaching them to observe all that I have commanded you."*
**—Matthew 28:19-20**

*The disciple of Christ must not only keep the faith and live on it, but also profess it, confidently bear witness to it, and spread it.*
**—CCC 1816**

## FIND IT

1. Following the battle, what does Aslan tell Lucy to do?

2. Why does Edmund's appearance change as the story progresses?

3. Aslan's providing food for everyone reminds us of which miracle performed by Christ?

4. Why does the White Stag appear at the end of the book?

5. Why does the Professor tell the children that they shouldn't seek to go back to Narnia?

## TALK IT OUT

1. The author tells us that Lucy's cordial is a reminder of holy chrism and Baptism. What are the similarities between the cordial and its effect on the wounded and the Oil of the Sick, which is used in the sacrament of the Anointing of the Sick, and its effect on those in danger of death? What are the differences?

2. What does it mean that a priest acts *in persona Christi*, especially when celebrating the sacraments? How should this affect our view of the priesthood?

3.  In a marked difference from Narnia, where Edmund wasn't told about Aslan's sacrifice, Christians are called to share the Good News that Jesus died for our sins. Why is it important for us to tell others that Christ suffered and died for us?

## ACTIVITY
### Wise Kings and Queens in Narnia

Imagine that you, like Peter, Susan, Edmund, and Lucy have stumbled into a different world and learn that you were chosen to be a king or queen of that land. Make a list of ten "good" laws that you would make to protect the citizens and to help everyone who lives there. In the alternative, make a list of ten "good" rules for your school, parish, or home that would promote harmony and help others.

## ACTIVITY
### Being an Effective Witness for Christ

Pope St. Paul VI said that "the first means of evangelization is the witness of an authentically Christian life" (*Evangelii Nuntiandi,* 41). In similar words, St. Francis reportedly said, "Preach the Gospel at all times, and when necessary use words." What were Pope St. Paul VI and St. Francis trying to say? What are things that we can do to live an "authentic Christian life" so as to be a better witness for Christ?

## FOR FURTHER EXPLORATION

What are the other books in *The Chronicles of Narnia*? Which book would you like to read next, and why?

# Acknowledgments

The following authors contributed to this book
*(listed alphabetically):*

Sue Allen

Tom Allen

Tommy Allen

Jeffrey Cole

Jennifer Cope

Michael Flickinger

Sara McLaughlin

Matthew Pinto

Mark Shea

The Editors of Catholic Exchange

Editorial and technical assistance by
Michael Fontecchio, Michael J. Miller,
Thomas A. Szyszkiewicz, and Lauren McCann.

# Appendix

| Question Number in *The Catholic Guide to Narnia* | Chapter in *The Lion, the Witch and the Wardrobe* by C.S. Lewis | Time Stamp in the Disney Movie *The Lion, the Witch and the Wardrobe* |
|---|---|---|
| Question No. 7 | Chapter 1 | 00:02:58 – 00:05:19 |
| Question No. 8 | Chapter 1 | 00:08:27 – 00:08:57 |
| Question No. 10 | Chapter 1 | 00:10:09 – 00:12:15 |
| Question No. 13 | Chapter 1 | 00:13:50 |
| Question No. 15 | Chapters 1 and 2 | 00:14:32 |
| Question No. 16 | Chapter 2 | 00:16:12 |
| Question No. 17 | Chapter 2 | 00:17:40 – 00:18:15 |
| Question No. 18 | Chapter 2 | |
| Question No. 20 | Chapter 2 | |
| Question No. 21 | Chapter 2 | |
| Question No. 24 | Chapter 2 | 00:22:20 – 00:24:28 |
| Question No. 25 | Chapter 3 | 00:24:36 – 00:25:07 |
| Question No. 26 | Chapter 3 | 00:27:58 – 00:28:30 |
| Question No. 27 | Chapter 3 | |
| Question No. 28 | Chapter 4 | 00:32:08 |
| Question No. 29 | Chapter 4 | 00:30:56; 00:32:36 |
| Question No. 30 | Chapter 4 | 00:33:42 |
| Question No. 31 | Chapter 4 | 00:33:00 |
| Question No. 32 | Chapter 4 | |

| | | |
|---|---|---|
| Question No. 33 | Chapter 5 | 00:35:42 |
| Question No. 34 | Chapter 5 | 00:35:22 |
| Question No. 35 | Chapter 5 | |
| Question No. 36 | Chapter 5 | 00:37:06 – 00:38:08 |
| Question No. 37 | Chapter 6 | |
| Question No. 40 | Chapter 6 | 00:43:37 |
| Question No. 41 | Chapter 7 | 00:48:03 |
| Question No. 42 | Chapter 8 | 00:48:14 – 00:49:40 |
| Question No. 43 | Chapter 8 | 00:48:32 |
| Question No. 44 | Chapter 8/13 | |
| Question No. 45 | Chapter 13 | |
| Question No. 46 | Chapter 8 | |
| Question No. 48 | Chapter 7 | 00:45:10 |
| Question No. 49 | Chapter 8 | 00:35:20 – 00:35:53; 00:44:00; 00:45:48 |
| Question No. 50 | Chapter 9 | 00:50:25 |
| Question No. 51 | Chapter 9 | |
| Question No. 53 | Chapter 10 | 01:08:42 – 01:11:07 |
| Question No. 54 | Chapter 10 | 01:09:38 – 01:11:07 |
| Question No. 55 | Chapter 11 | 01:17:55 – 01:18:48 |
| Question No. 56 | Chapter 11 | |
| Question No. 57 | Chapter 11 | 01:48:48 |
| Question No. 58 | Chapters 13 and 14 | |
| Question No. 59 | Chapter 13 | 00:43:08 – 00:43:30; 00:56:11 |
| Question No. 60 | Chapter 12 | 01:19:00 – 01:20:25 |
| Question No. 61 | Chapter 12 | |

| | | |
|---|---|---|
| Question No. 62 | Chapter 12 | |
| Question No. 63 | Chapter 12 | |
| Question No. 64 | Chapter 13 | |
| Question No. 65 | Chapter 13 | 01:23:40 – 01:24:00 |
| Question No. 66 | Chapter 13 | 01:27:05 |
| Question No. 67 | Chapter 12 | 01:25:07 – 01:26:30 |
| Question No. 68 | Chapter 13 | 01:28:09 – 01:29:05 |
| Question No. 69 | Chapter 13 | 01:29:10 – 01:29:55 |
| Question No. 70 | Chapter 13 | 01:33:38 |
| Question No. 71 | Chapter 14 | |
| Question No. 73 | Chapter 14 | |
| Question No. 74 | Chapter 13 | 01:32:05 – 01:32:25 |
| Question No. 75 | Chapter 13 | 01:32:30 |
| Question No. 76 | Chapter 13 | |
| Question No. 77 | Chapter 12 | 01:33:20 |
| Question No. 79 | Chapter 13 | 01:32:43 |
| Question No. 80 | Chapter 13 | 01:32:35 – 01:32:43 |
| Question No. 81 | Chapter 15 | |
| Question No. 82 | Chapter 14 | |
| Question No. 84 | Chapter 14 | 01:37:15 – 01:45:25;<br>01:52:41 – 01:54:41 |
| Question No. 86 | Chapter 15 | 01:53:28 – 01:54:41 |
| Question No. 87 | Chapter 15 | 01:54:25 |
| Question No. 89 | Chapter 15 | |
| Question No. 90 | Chapter 15 | 01:53:28 |
| Question No. 91 | Chapter 16 | 01:58:45 – 01:59:30 |

| | | |
|---|---|---|
| Question No. 92 | Chapter 16 | |
| Question No. 93 | Chapter 17 | 02:04:02 – 02:05:20 |
| Question No. 94 | Chapter 17 | |
| Question No. 95 | Chapter 17 | |
| Question No. 96 | Chapter 17 | |
| Question No. 97 | Chapter 17 | 02:09:07 – 02:11:00 |
| Question No. 99 | Chapter 17 | 02:12:15 – 02:13:20 |
| Question No. 100 | Chapter 17 | 02:11:00 – 02:11:35 |